RESUMES
FOR
ENGINEERING
CAREERS

Professional Resumes Series

RESUMES
FOR
ENGINEERING
CAREERS

The Editors of
VGM Career Horizons

Printed on recyclable paper

VGM Career Horizons
a division of *NTC Publishing Group*
Lincolnwood, Illinois USA

ACKNOWLEDGMENT

We would like to acknowledge the assistance of Cheryl McLean in compiling and editing this book.

Library of Congress Cataloging-in-Publication Data

Resumes for engineering careers/the editors of VGM Career Horizons.

   p. cm.
   ISBN 0–8442-4160-1
   1. Engineers—Employment. 2. Résumés (Employment) I. VGM Career
Horizons (Firm)
TA157.R47 1994   93-45474
808'.06665–dc20   CIP

1995 Printing

CONTENTS

Introduction

Your resume is your first impression on a prospective employer. Though you may be articulate, intelligent, and charming in person, a poor resume may prevent you from ever having the opportunity to demonstrate your interpersonal skills, because a poor resume may prevent you from ever being called for an interview. While few people have ever been hired solely on the basis of their resume, a well-written, well-organized resume can go a long way toward helping you land an interview. Your resume's main purpose is to get you that interview. The rest is up to you and the employer. If you both feel that you are right for the job and the job is right for you, chances are you will be hired.

A resume must catch the reader's attention yet still be easy to read and to the point. Resume styles have changed over the years. Today, brief and focused resumes are preferred. No longer do employers have the patience, or the time, to review several pages of solid type. A resume should be only one page long, if possible, and never more than two pages. Time is a precious commodity in today's business world and the resume that is concise and straightforward will usually be the one that gets noticed.

Let's not make the mistake, though, of assuming that writing a brief resume means that you can take less care in preparing it. A successful resume takes time and thought, and if you are willing to make the effort, the rewards are well worth it. Think of your resume as a sales tool with the product being you. You want to sell yourself to a prospective employer. This book is designed to help you prepare a resume that will help you further your career—to land that next job, or first job, or to return to the work force after years of absence. So, read on. Make the effort and reap the rewards that a strong resume can bring to your career. Let's get to it!

Chapter One

THE ELEMENTS OF A GOOD RESUME

A winning resume is made of the elements that employers are most interested in seeing when reviewing a job applicant. These basic elements are the essential ingredients of a successful resume and become the actual sections of your resume. The following is a list of elements that may be used in a resume. Some are essential; some are optional. We will be discussing these in this chapter in order to give you a better understanding of each element's role in the makeup of your resume:

1. Heading
2. Objective
3. Work Experience
4. Education
5. Honors
6. Activities
7. Certificates and Licenses
8. Professional Memberships
9. Special Skills
10. Personal Information
11. References

The first step in preparing your resume is to gather together information about yourself and your past accomplishments. Later you will refine this information, rewrite it in the most effective language, and organize it into the most attractive layout. First, let's take a look at each of these important elements individually.

Heading

The heading may seem to be a simple enough element in your resume, but be careful not to take it lightly. The heading should be placed at the top of your resume and should include your name, home address, and telephone numbers. If you can take calls at your current place of business, include your business number, since most employers will attempt to contact you during the business day. If this is not possible, or if you can afford it, purchase an answering machine that allows you to retrieve your messages while you are away from home. This way you can make sure you don't miss important phone calls. *Always* include your phone number on your resume. It is crucial that when prospective employers need to have immediate contact with you, they can.

Objective

When seeking a particular career path, it is important to list a job objective on your resume. This statement helps employers know the direction that you see yourself heading, so that they can determine whether your goals are in line with the position available. The objective is normally one sentence long and describes your employment goals clearly and concisely. See the sample resumes in this book for examples of objective statements.

The job objective will vary depending on the type of person you are, the field you are in, and the type of goals you have. It can be either specific or general, but it should always be to the point.

In some cases, this element is not necessary, but usually it is a good idea to include your objective. It gives your possible future employer an idea of where you are coming from and where you want to go.

The objective statement is better left out, however, if you are uncertain of the exact title of the job you seek. In such a case, the inclusion of an overly specific objective statement could result in your not being considered for a variety of acceptable positions; you should be sure to incorporate this information in your cover letter, instead.

Work Experience

This element is arguably the most important of them all. It will provide the central focus of your resume, so it is necessary that this section be as complete as possible. Only by examining your work experience in depth can you get to the heart of your accomplishments and present them in a way that demonstrates the strength of your qualifications. Of course, someone just out of school will have less work experience than someone who has been working for a number of years, but the amount of information isn't the most important thing—rather, how it is presented and how it highlights you as a person and as a worker will be what counts.

As you work on this section of your resume, be aware of the need for accuracy. You'll want to include all necessary information about each of your jobs, including job title, dates, employer, city, state, responsibilities, special projects, and accomplishments. Be sure to only list company accomplishments for which you were directly responsible. If you haven't participated in any special projects, that's all right—this area may not be relevant to certain jobs.

The most common way to list your work experience is in *reverse chronological order*. In other words, start with your most recent job and work your way backwards. This way your prospective employer sees your current (and often most important) job before seeing your past jobs. Your most recent position, if the most important, should also be the one that includes the most information, as compared to your previous positions. If you are just out of school, show your summer employment and part-time work, though in this case your education will most likely be more important than your work experience.

The following worksheets will help you gather information about your past jobs.

WORK EXPERIENCE
Job One:

Job Title _____

Dates _____

Employer _____

City, State _____

Major Duties _____

_____

_____

_____

_____

_____

_____

_____

Special Projects _____

_____

_____

_____

Accomplishments _____

_____

_____

_____

_____

_____

_____

_____

_____

Job Two:

Job Title _____

Dates _____

Employer _____

City, State _____

Major Duties _____

_____

_____

_____

_____

_____

_____

_____

Special Projects _____

_____

_____

_____

Accomplishments _____

_____

_____

_____

_____

_____

_____

_____

Job Three:

Job Title _____

Dates _____

Employer _____

City, State _____

Major Duties _____

_____

_____

_____

_____

_____

_____

_____

Special Projects _____

_____

_____

_____

Accomplishments _____

_____

_____

_____

_____

_____

_____

_____

_____

Job Four:

Job Title _____

Dates _____

Employer _____

City, State _____

Major Duties _____

_____

_____

_____

_____

_____

_____

Special Projects _____

_____

_____

_____

Accomplishments _____

_____

_____

_____

_____

_____

_____

_____

_____

Education

Education is the second most important element of a resume. Your educational background is often a deciding factor in an employer's decision to hire you. Be sure to stress your accomplishments in school with the same finesse that you stressed your accomplishments at work. If you are looking for your first job, your education will be your greatest asset, since your work experience will most likely be minimal. In this case, the education section becomes the most important. You will want to be sure to include any degrees or certificates you received, your major area of concentration, any honors, and any relevant activities. Again, be sure to list your most recent schooling first. If you have completed graduate-level work, begin with that and work in reverse chronological order through your undergraduate education. If you have completed an undergraduate degree, you may choose whether to list your high school experience or not. This should be done only if your high school grade-point average was well above average.

The following worksheets will help you gather information for this section of your resume. Also included are supplemental worksheets for honors and for activities. Sometimes honors and activities are listed in a section separate from education, most often near the end of the resume.

EDUCATION

School _____

Major or Area of Concentration _____

Degree _____

Date _____

School _____

Major or Area of Concentration _____

Degree _____

Date _____

Honors

Here, you should list any awards, honors, or memberships in honorary societies that you have received. Usually these are of an academic nature, but they can also be for special achievement in sports, clubs, or other school activities. Always be sure to include the name of the organization honoring you and the date(s) received. Use the worksheet below to help gather your honors information.

HONORS

Honor: _____

Awarding Organization: _____

Date(s): _____

Honor: _____

Awarding Organization: _____

Date(s): _____

Honor: _____

Awarding Organization: _____

Date(s): _____

Honor: _____

Awarding Organization: _____

Date(s): _____

Activities

You may have been active in different organizations or clubs during your years at school; often an employer will look at such involvement as evidence of initiative and dedication. Your ability to take an active role, and even a leadership role, in a group should be included on your resume. Use the worksheet provided to list your activities and accomplishments in this area. In general, you should exclude any organization the name of which indicates the race, creed, sex, age, marital status, color, or nation of origin of its members.

ACTIVITIES

Organization/Activity: _____

Accomplishments: _____

_____

_____

Organization/Activity: _____

Accomplishments: _____

_____

_____

Organization/Activity: _____

Accomplishments: _____

_____

_____

Organization/Activity: _____

Accomplishments: _____

_____

_____

As your work experience increases through the years, your school activities and honors will play less of a role in your resume, and eventually you will most likely only list your degree and any major honors you received. This is due to the fact that, as time goes by, your job performance becomes the most important element in your resume. Through time, your resume should change to reflect this.

Certificates and Licenses

The next potential element of your resume is certificates and licenses. You should list these if the job you are seeking requires them and you, of course, have acquired them. If you have applied for a license, but have not yet received it, use the phrase "application pending."

License requirements vary by state. If you have moved or you are planning to move to another state, be sure to check with the appropriate board or licensing agency in the state in which you are applying for work to be sure that you are aware of all licensing requirements.

Always be sure that all of the information you list is completely accurate. Locate copies of your licenses and certificates and check the exact date and name of the accrediting agency. Use the following worksheet to list your licenses and certificates.

CERTIFICATES AND LICENSES

Name of License: _____

Licensing Agency: _____

Date Issued: _____

Name of License: _____

Licensing Agency: _____

Date Issued: _____

Name of License: _____

Licensing Agency: _____

Date Issued: _____

Professional Memberships

Another potential element in your resume is a section listing professional memberships. Use this section to list involvement in professional associations, unions, and similar organizations. It is to your advantage to list any professional memberships that pertain to the job you are seeking. Be sure to include the dates of your involvement and whether you took part in any special activities or held any offices within the organization. Use the following worksheet to gather your information.

PROFESSIONAL MEMBERSHIPS

Name of Organization: _____

Offices Held: _____

Activities: _____

Date(s): _____

Name of Organization: _____

Offices Held: _____

Activities: _____

Date(s): _____

Name of Organization: _____

Offices Held: _____

Activities: _____

Date(s): _____

Name of Organization: _____

Offices Held: _____

Activities: _____

Date(s): _____

Special Skills

This section of your resume is set aside for mentioning any special abilities you have that could relate to the job you are seeking. This is the part of your resume where you have the opportunity to demonstrate certain talents and experiences that are not necessarily a part of your educational or work experience. Common examples include fluency in a foreign language, or knowledge of a particular computer application.

Special skills can encompass a wide range of your talents—remember to be sure that whatever skills you list relate to the type of work you are looking for.

Personal Information

Some people include "Personal" information on their resumes. This is not generally recommended, but you might wish to include it if you think that something in your personal life, such as a hobby or talent, has some bearing on the position you are seeking. This type of information is often referred to at the beginning of an interview, when it is used as an "ice breaker." Of course, personal information regarding age, marital status, race, religion, or sexual preference should never appear on any resume.

References

References are not usually listed on the resume, but a prospective employer needs to know that you have references who may be contacted if necessary. All that is necessary to include in your resume regarding references is a sentence at the bottom stating, "References are available upon request." If a prospective employer requests a list of references, be sure to have one ready. Also, check with whomever you list to see if it is all right for you to use them as a reference. Forewarn them that they may receive a call regarding a reference for you. This way they can be prepared to give you the best reference possible.

Chapter Two

WRITING YOUR RESUME

*N*ow that you have gathered together all of the information for each of the sections of your resume, it's time to write out each section in a way that will get the attention of whoever is reviewing it. The type of language you use in your resume will affect its success. You want to take the information you have gathered and translate it into a language that will cause a potential employer to sit up and take notice.

Resume writing is not like expository writing or creative writing. It embodies a functional, direct writing style and focuses on the use of action words. By using action words in your writing, you more effectively stress past accomplishments. Action words help demonstrate your initiative and highlight your talents. Always use verbs that show strength and reflect the qualities of a "doer." By using action words, you characterize yourself as a person who takes action, and this will impress potential employers.

The following is a list of verbs commonly used in resume writing. Use this list to choose the action words that can help your resume become a strong one:

administered

advised

analyzed

arranged

assembled

assumed responsibility

billed

built

carried out

channeled

collected

communicated

compiled

completed

conducted

contacted

contracted

coordinated

counseled

created

cut

designed

determined

developed

directed

dispatched

distributed

documented

edited

established

expanded

functioned as

gathered

handled

hired

implemented

improved

inspected

interviewed

introduced

invented

maintained

managed

met with

motivated

negotiated

operated

orchestrated

ordered

organized

oversaw

performed

planned

prepared

presented

produced

programmed

published

purchased

recommended

recorded

reduced

referred

represented

researched

reviewed

saved

screened

served as

served on

sold

suggested

supervised

taught

tested

trained

typed

wrote

Now take a look at the information you put down on the work experience worksheets. Take that information and rewrite it in paragraph form, using verbs to highlight your actions and accomplishments. Let's look at an example, remembering that what matters here is the writing style, and not the particular job responsibilities given in our sample.

WORK EXPERIENCE
Regional Sales Manager

Manager of sales representatives from seven states. Responsible for twelve food chain accounts in the East. In charge of directing the sales force in planned selling toward specific goals. Supervisor and trainer of new sales representatives. Consulting for customers in the areas of inventory management and quality control.

Special Projects: Coordinator and sponsor of annual food industry sales seminar.

Accomplishments: Monthly regional volume went up 25 percent during my tenure while, at the same time, a proper sales/cost ratio was maintained. Customer/company relations improved significantly.

Below is the rewritten version of this information, using action words. Notice how much stronger it sounds.

WORK EXPERIENCE
Regional Sales Manager

Managed sales representatives from seven states. Handled twelve food chain accounts in the eastern United States. Directed the sales force in planned selling towards specific goals. Supervised and trained new sales representatives. Consulted for customers in the areas of inventory management and quality control. Coordinated and sponsored the annual Food Industry Seminar. Increased monthly regional volume 25 percent and helped to improve customer/company relations during my tenure.

Another way of constructing the work experience section is by using actual job descriptions. Job descriptions are rarely written using the proper resume language, but they do include all the information necessary to create this section of your resume. Take the description of one of the jobs your are including on your resume (if you have access to it), and turn it into an action-oriented paragraph. Below is an example of a job description followed by a version of the same description written using action words. Again, pay attention to the style of writing, as the details of your own work experience will be unique.

PUBLIC ADMINISTRATOR I

Responsibilities: Coordinate and direct public services to meet the needs of the nation, state, or community. Analyze problems; work with special committees and public agencies; recommend solutions to governing bodies.

Aptitudes and Skills: Ability to relate to and communicate with people; solve complex problems through analysis; plan, organize, and implement policies and programs. Knowledge of political systems; financial management; personnel administration; program evaluation; organizational theory.

WORK EXPERIENCE
Public Administrator I

Wrote pamphlets and conducted discussion groups to inform citizens of legislative processes and consumer issues. Organized and supervised 25 interviewers. Trained interviewers in effective communication skills.

Now that you have learned how to word your resume, you are ready for the next step in your quest for a winning resume: assembly and layout.

Chapter Three

ASSEMBLY AND LAYOUT

*A*t this point, you've gathered all the necessary information for your resume, and you've rewritten it using the language necessary to impress potential employers. Your next step is to assemble these elements in a logical order and then to lay them out on the page neatly and attractively in order to achieve the desired effect: getting that interview.

Assembly

The order of the elements in a resume makes a difference in its overall effect. Obviously, you would not want to put your name and address in the middle of the resume or your special skills section at the top. You want to put the elements in an order that stresses your most important achievements, not the less pertinent information. For example, if you recently graduated from school and have no full-time work experience, you will want to list your education before you list any part-time jobs you may have held during school. On the other hand, if you have been gainfully employed for several years and currently hold an important position in your company, you will want to list your work experience ahead of your education, which has become less pertinent with time.

There are some elements that are always included in your resume and some that are optional. Following is a list of essential and optional elements:

Essential	*Optional*
Name	Job Objective
Address	Honors
Phone Number	Special Skills
Work Experience	Professional Memberships
Education	Activities
References Phrase	Certificates and Licenses
	Personal Information

Your choice of optional sections depends on your own background and employment needs. Always use information that will put you and your abilities in a favorable light. If your honors are impressive, then be sure to include them in your resume. If your activities in school demonstrate particular talents necessary for the job you are seeking, then allow space for a section on activities. Each resume is unique, just as each person is unique.

Types of Resumes

So far, our discussion about resumes has involved the most common type—the *reverse chronological* resume, in which your most recent job is listed first and so on. This is the type of resume usually preferred by human resources directors, and it is the one most frequently used. However, in some cases this style of presentation is not the most effective way to highlight your skills and accomplishments.

For someone reentering the work force after many years or someone looking to change career fields, the *functional resume* may work best. This type of resume focuses more on achievement and less on the sequence of your work history. In the functional resume, your experience is presented by what you have accomplished and the skills you have developed in your past work.

A functional resume can be assembled from the same information you collected for your chronological resume. The main difference lies in how you organize this information. Essentially, the work experience section becomes two sections, with your job duties and accomplishments comprising one section and your employer's name, city, state, your position, and the dates employed making up another section. The first section is placed near the top of the resume, just below the job objective section, and can be called *Accomplishments* or *Achievements*. The second section, containing the bare essentials of your employment history, should come after the accomplishments section and can be titled *Work Experience* or *Employment History*. The other sections of your resume remain the same. The work experience section is the only one affected in the functional resume. By placing the section that focuses on your achievements first, you thereby draw attention to these achievements. This puts less emphasis on who you worked for and more emphasis on what you did and what you are capable of doing.

For someone changing careers, emphasis on skills and achievements is essential. The identities of previous employers, which may be unrelated to one's new job field, need to be downplayed. The functional resume accomplishes this task. For someone reentering the work force after many years, a functional resume is the obvious choice. If you lack full-time work experience, you will need to draw attention away from this fact and instead focus on your skills and abilities gained possibly through volunteer activities or part-time work. Education may also play a more important role in this resume.

Which type of resume is right for you will depend on your own personal circumstances. It may be helpful to create a chronological *and* a functional resume and then compare the two to find out which is more suitable. The sample resumes found in this book include both chronological and functional resumes. Use these resumes as guides to help you decide on the content and appearance of your own resume.

Layout

Once you have decided which elements to include in your resume and you have arranged them in an order that makes sense and emphasizes your achievements and abilities, then it is time to work on the physical layout of your resume.

There is no single appropriate layout that applies to every resume, but there are a few basic rules to follow in putting your resume on paper:

1. Leave a comfortable margin on the sides, top, and bottom of the page (usually 1 to 1¹/₂ inches).

2. Use appropriate spacing between the sections (usually 2 to 3 line spaces are adequate).

3. Be consistent in the *type* of headings you use for the different sections of your resume. For example, if you capitalize the heading EMPLOYMENT HISTORY, don't use initial capitals and underlining for a heading of equal importance, such as Education.

4. Always try to fit your resume onto one page. If you are having trouble fitting all your information onto one page, perhaps you are trying to say too much. Try to edit out any repetitive or unnecessary information or possibly shorten descriptions of earlier jobs. Be ruthless. Maybe you've included too many optional sections.

CHRONOLOGICAL RESUME

DAVON X. DESOTO
22 NE 56th Street
Pittsburgh, PA 15244
412-555-3742

OBJECTIVE

A supervisory/management position with an engineering firm that will challenge and enhance my experience, knowledge, skills and years of increasing responsibility.

HIGHLIGHTS OF QUALIFICATIONS

Twenty-three years of engineering, management and supervisory experience in managing facilities, equipment and personnel. Supervision of over 100 personnel. Extensive skills in planning, coordinating and supervising of projects. Reliable and adaptable; learn new systems quickly, and take initiative. Able to represent company with a professional appearance and manner.

WORK EXPERIENCE

Operation Supervisor, Suver Pennsylvania Compost Company, Inc. 1980-present.
Controlled entire plant operations of a 600 ton-per-day MSW facility with 100 employees. Assumed full responsibilities in absence of plant manager. Responsible for interviewing and hiring of employees, work schedules, daily production and technical inspections of equipment. Fully involved in daily performance testing. Provided training to all personnel.

Superintendent, Suver Waste Systems, Kingley Fast Disposal. 1976-1980.
Assumed responsibility of closure of KFD Landfill. Coordinated employee work schedules for ten personnel; truck delivery of closure material; work schedules of subcontractors tasked with installation of PVC liner. Economically solved soil erosion problems. Scheduled maintenance for and operated heavy equipment. Made purchases as needed for daily operations.

Group Engineer, Commissioned Chief Warrant Officer, USCG. 1972-1976.
Responsible for the direction of all civil and naval engineering support. Direct and indirect supervision of over 100 personnel for the maintenance of large patrol boats, small boats, Coast Guard facilities, including various duty stations and 97 housing units. Responsible for personnel training and budget management and procurement for a department with a budget of $250,000 annually and individual contracts in excess of $80,000. Other assigned duties included Safety Officer, Hazardous Waste Officer and Energy Conservation Coordinator.

Group Engineer, Senior Chief Machinery Technician, USCG. 1970-1972.
Responsible for the management and maintenance of two Coast Guard stations, two large patrol boats and several small boats, including electrical, propulsion and hydraulic systems. Responsible for development of computerized maintenance project list, budget administration and supervision of over 50 personnel.

FUNCTIONAL RESUME

RAY-DEAN BENNETT
15543 Framington Lane
Walnut Creek, California 94595
(415) 555-0928

PROFESSIONAL OBJECTIVE

Design engineering in robotics automation for manufacturing.

EDUCATION

BSME, Mechanical Engineering, California Institute of Technology, 1993
BSEE, Electrical Engineering, California Institute of Technology, 1992

EXPERIENCE/SKILLS

• Strong mechanical and electrical engineering background, with course and lab emphasis in robotics and production-related problem solving.

• Extra coursework in heat sensing, CAD/CAM design, electronic control systems, computer programming (COBOL, PASCAL, BASIC), and image-enhancing technology.

• Won regional mechanical engineering competition for design of robotics manufacturing station for production of small motor.

• Extensive knowledge of automotive mechanics and related machinery. Worked in family-owned automotive repair shop for 8 years, including complete engine rebuilding and overhaul.

• Experienced with use of personal computers for design, word processing, database management, and spreadsheet functions.

MEMBERSHIPS
Student chapter of the IEEE and IAME • Tau Kappa Epsilon Honor Society

EMPLOYMENT HISTORY

Bennett's Auto Experts, Engine Mechanic, 1984-1992

REFERENCES

Available upon request

Don't let the idea of having to tell every detail about your life get in the way of producing a resume that is simple and straightforward. The more compact your resume, the easier it will be to read and the better an impression it will make for you.

In some cases, the resume will not fit on a single page, even after extensive editing. In such cases, the resume should be printed on two pages so as not to compromise clarity or appearance. Each page of a two-page resume should be marked clearly with your name and the page number, e.g., "Judith Ramirez, page 1 of 2." The pages should then be stapled together.

Try experimenting with various layouts until you find one that looks good to you. Always show your final layout to other people and ask them what they like or dislike about it, and what impresses them most about your resume. Make sure that is what you want most to emphasize. If it isn't, you may want to consider making changes in your layout until the necessary information is emphasized. Use the sample resumes in this book to get some ideas for laying out your resume.

Putting Your Resume in Print

Your resume should be typed or printed on good quality 8½″ × 11″ bond paper. You want to make as good an impression as possible with your resume; therefore, quality paper is a necessity. If you have access to a word processor with a good printer, or know of someone who does, make use of it. Typewritten resumes should only be used when there are no other options available.

After you have produced a clean original, you will want to make duplicate copies of it. Usually a copy shop is your best bet for producing copies without smudges or streaks. Make sure you have the copy shop use quality bond paper for all copies of your resume. Ask for a sample copy before they run your entire order. After copies are made, check each copy for cleanliness and clarity.

Another more costly option is to have your resume typeset and printed by a printer. This will provide the most attractive resume of all. If you anticipate needing a lot of copies of your resume, the cost of having it typeset may be justified.

Proofreading

After you have finished typing the master copy of your resume and before you go to have it copied or printed, you must thoroughly check it for typing and spelling errors. Have several people read it over just in case you may have missed an error. Misspelled words and typing mistakes will not make a good impression on a prospective employer, as they are a bad reflection on your writing ability and your attention to detail. With thorough and conscientious proofreading, these mistakes can be avoided.

The following are some rules of capitalization and punctuation that may come in handy when proofreading your resume:

Rules of Capitalization

- Capitalize proper nouns, such as names of schools, colleges, and universities, names of companies, and brand names of products.

- Capitalize major words in the names and titles of books, tests, and articles that appear in the body of your resume.

- Capitalize words in major section headings of your resume.

- Do not capitalize words just because they seem important.

- When in doubt, consult a manual of style such as *Words Into Type* (Prentice-Hall), or *The Chicago Manual of Style* (The University of Chicago Press). Your local library can help you locate these and other reference books.

Rules of Punctuation

- Use a comma to separate words in a series.

- Use a semicolon to separate series of words that already include commas within the series.

- Use a semicolon to separate independent clauses that are not joined by a conjunction.

- Use a period to end a sentence.

- Use a colon to show that the examples or details that follow expand or amplify the preceding phrase.

- Avoid the use of dashes.

- Avoid the use of brackets.

- If you use any punctuation in an unusual way in your resume, be consistent in its use.

- Whenever you are uncertain, consult a style manual.

Chapter Four

THE COVER LETTER

*O*nce your resume has been assembled, laid out, and printed to your satisfaction, the next and final step before distribution is to write your cover letter. Though there may be instances where you deliver your resume in person, most often you will be sending it through the mail. Resumes sent through the mail always need an accompanying letter that briefly introduces you and your resume. The purpose of the cover letter is to get a potential employer to read your resume, just as the purpose of your resume is to get that same potential employer to call you for an interview.

Like your resume, your cover letter should be clean, neat, and direct. A cover letter usually includes the following information:

1. Your name and address (unless it already appears on your personal letterhead).

2. The date.

3. The name and address of the person and company to whom you are sending your resume.

4. The salutation ("Dear Mr." or "Dear Ms." followed by the person's last name, or "To Whom It May Concern" if you are answering a blind ad).

5. An opening paragraph explaining why you are writing (in response to an ad, the result of a previous meeting, at the suggestion of someone you both know) and indicating that you are interested in whatever job is being offered.

6. One or two more paragraphs that tell why you want to work for the company and what qualifications and experience you can bring to that company.

7. A final paragraph that closes the letter and requests that you be contacted for an interview. You may mention here that your references are available upon request.

8. The closing ("Sincerely," or "Yours Truly," followed by your signature with your name typed under it).

Your cover letter, including all of the information above, should be no more than one page in length. The language used should be polite, businesslike, and to the point. Do not attempt to tell your life story in the cover letter. A long and cluttered letter will only serve to put off the reader. Remember, you only need to mention a few of your accomplishments and skills in the cover letter. The rest of your information is in your resume. Each and every achievement should not be mentioned twice. If your cover letter is a success, your resume will be read and all pertinent information reviewed by your prospective employer.

Producing the Cover Letter

Cover letters should always be typed individually, since they are always written to particular individuals and companies. Never use a form letter for your cover letter. Cover letters cannot be copied or reproduced like resumes. Each one should be as personal as possible. Of course, once you have written and rewritten your first cover letter to the point where you are satisfied with it, you certainly can use similar wording in subsequent letters.

After you have typed your cover letter on quality bond paper, be sure to proofread it as thoroughly as you did your resume. Again, spelling errors are a sure sign of carelessness, and you don't want that to be a part of your first impression on a prospective employer. Make sure to handle the letter and resume carefully to avoid any smudges, and then mail both your cover letter and resume in an appropriate sized envelope. Be sure to keep an accurate record of all the resumes you send out and the results of each mailing, either in a separate notebook or on individual 3 × 5″ index cards.

Numerous sample cover letters appear at the end of the book. Use them as models for your own cover letter or to get an idea of how cover letters are put together. Remember, every one is unique and depends on the particular circumstances of the individual writing it and the job for which he or she is applying.

Now the job of writing your resume and cover letter is complete. About a week after mailing resumes and cover letters to potential employers, you will want to contact them by telephone. Confirm that your resume arrived, and ask whether an interview might be possible. Getting your foot in the door during this call is half the battle of a job search, and a strong resume and cover letter will help you immeasurably.

Chapter Five

SAMPLE RESUMES

This chapter contains dozens of sample resumes for people pursuing a wide variety of jobs and careers within this field.

There are many different styles of resumes in terms of graphic layout and presentation of information. These samples also represent people with varying amounts of education and work experience. Use these samples to model your own resume after. Choose one resume, or borrow elements from several different resumes to help you construct your own.

HUNTER BOTTJER

2254 W. Brick Street, Apt. B4 • Anchorage, AK 99510 • 907/555-2247

PROFESSIONAL OBJECTIVE

To achieve a associate-level management position in the drafting department of a major mechanical engineering firm.

EXPERIENCE

Assistant Manager, Product Engineering, Drafting Division, Aleutian-Pacific Engineering, Inc. Anchorage, Alaska • June 1990 to present

Supervise production drafting of engine parts for large-engine manufacturing company. Responsible for assessing and approving the quality of drafting by 14 full-time drafters. Saved the company $1.2 million in projected revenue loss by detecting design flaw in a major engine component.

Senior Drafter, Product Engineering, Drafting Division, Aleutian-Pacific Engineering, Inc. Anchorage, Alaska • April 1988 to June 1990

Drafting high-voltage power switching equipment to customer specifications and structures. Responsible for drafting component of major engine redesign in team-managed project. Drafter I & Drafter II • June 1981 to April 1988

Assistant Manager, Winter Creek Building Supply
Galena, Alaska • February 1977 to September 1979
Assisted in start-up of building supply firm in retail and wholesale sales, government sales, purchasing, and inventory control.

EDUCATION

Associate's Degree, Mechanical Engineering
Kitsap Community College
Kitsap, Washington • June 1981

REFERENCES AVAILABLE

Brenda Harwood
26587 S.E. Wynona Drive
Casa Grande, Arizona 85223
(602) 555-2910

PROFESSIONAL GOAL
To work in the drafting department of a mechanical engineering firm.

EXPERIENCE

Hyster Company, Casa Grande, Arizona
Drafter
May 1989 to present

> Skilled in general production and maintenance drafting, cost reduction research, and design-phase drafting. Work closely with designers to refine plans. Assist senior drafters with checking of drawings, preparing and releasing engineering change notices, managing department inventory, and monitoring production lists.

Engineering Assistant
July 1986 to May 1989

> Assisted engineers with preparing detailed instructions for drafting department, including product design specifications, material specifications, and documentation. Consulted with drafters on design and engineering changes. Maintained detailed records of all inter-departmental communications for each specific project.

EDUCATION

Arizona State University
Mechanical Drawing/Industrial Design
B.S. 1986

> Won honorable mention in competition for the design of a small-scale turbine .

REFERENCES AVAILABLE ON REQUEST

Darryl H. Wynston
944 West Saska Boulevard, Bridgeport, Alabama 35740
(205) 555-3985

OBJECTIVE
To work as a mechanical designer or drafter for a company that offers professional advancement.

EXPERIENCE
Senior Drafter
Bennington Mechanics Handling Corp., Montgomery, Alabama
5/90 - present
Prepare primary and secondary concept layouts, component layouts, complex assembly drawings, and parts drawings. Prepare and release engineering change notices and production lists.

Product Engineering Drafter
General Metals Products, Montgomery, Alabama
6/80 - 5/90
Draft architectural sheet metal products designs to customer specifications. Check mechanical drawings for accuracy and precision. Maintain drafting files for product engineering department.

ACCOMPLISHMENTS
Used Computervision CADD System for design and layout work on a new power shift transmission.
Developed prototype for H350-2LX noise reduction feature for major engine product.
Experienced with CS-4x Revision 6.2b, 3-D and solids.
Computervision CADD operator since 7/87.

EDUCATION
Major in Mechanical Engineering
Montgomery Regional Technical Institute
9/78 - 6/80
Completed 108 credit hours toward B.S. degree

REFERENCES
Available on request

TERRY WILKINS, JR. • 132 East Park St. • Jacksonville, Arkansas 72076 • (501) 555-0983

PROFESSIONAL OBJECTIVE

Seeking a position of responsibility in mechanical engineering. Willing to relocate.

PROFILE OF QUALIFICATIONS

Offering over 13 years of professional experience in mechanical engineering, with particular emphasis in:

- Dimension checking
- Bills of materials
- Layout/drawing
- Interdepartmental communication
- Metric drafting standards

- Material specifications
- Engineering records
- Manufacturing processes
- Documentation
- Computer-aided design and drafting

EDUCATION

Associate of Applied Science in Mechanical Drafting Technology, 1975
• Little Rock Central Community College, Little Rock, Arkansas

Bachelor of Arts in History, 1969
• University of Arkansas, Little Rock

RELATED CAREER HIGHLIGHTS

JEPSON CORPORATION, Jacksonville, Arkansas
• ENGINEERING CHANGE NOTICE CHECKER: 1988-present

Responsible for checking all engineering drawings for dimensional accuracy, correct material specifications, correct drafting procedures, and accuracy of accompanying bills of material. Maintain scheduled release dates and ensure that all production processes can be carried out expeditiously.

• ENGINEERING DRAFTSMAN: 1977-1988

Prepared layouts and drawings of new and existing industrial truck products. Work included component layouts, details, general arrangement drawings, and more. Consulted with departmental engineers and purchasing personnel. Accompanied work with documentation.

U.S. DEPARTMENT OF TRANSPORTATION, Little Rock, Arkansas
• ENGINEERING AIDE (GS-3): 1975-1977

Assisted departmental engineers with drafting and documentation.

REFERENCES AVAILABLE

KEVIN SHANNON

P.O. Box 231, Bakersfield, CA 93301 / 805-555-9721

OBJECTIVE

Relocating to Los Angeles; seeking challenging employment with industrial engineering department of a large manufacturing company.

EDUCATION

A.A.S., Applied Engineering, 1978
College of Applied Technology, Los Angeles

Continuing Education coursework (36 hours)
Bakersfield Technical College, 1982-1992

ACCOMPLISHMENTS

Named National Coordinator for corporation's P.A.R. system (Parts Action Request), which was an internal method of relaying information to manufacturer, purchasing, and others.

Instrumental in procedural change, using engineering drawings in lieu of sketches for the installation of customer-requested options not found on standard bills of material.

Approve or reject engineering design variation requests, ensuring that appropriate changes comply with specifications and structural requirements.

Provided bills of material, worked with component vendors to secure special parts inventory, and compiled installation layouts.

Responsible for training new employees in engineering drafting practices and standards.

Coordinate employee re-training program through local technical college.

Developed and implemented safety program that resulted in a 35% decrease in on-the-job injuries.

EXPERIENCE

Industrial Manufacturing, Inc., Bakersfield, CA
    Departmental Coordinator, Parts Engineering / Dec. 1988-present
    Assistant Supervisor / 1983-1988
    Engineering Aide / 1978-1983

REFERENCES AVAILABLE

SUSAN B. WATTERS-LEVY

Current Address (until May 30):   Permanent Address:
3329 West 52nd Avenue   P.O. Box 15384
Denton, Texas 77402   San Antonio, Texas 78231
(713) 555-2975

OBJECTIVE:
Electronic engineering position involving design, manufacture, and testing of digital control systems.

EDUCATION:
BSEE (May 1994), West Texas State University, Canyonville
EE GPA, 4.0; Cumulative GPA, 3.56. Dean's List.

RELATED EXPERIENCE:
Laboratory Technician/Research Assistant, Department of Electrical Engineering. 1993-94. Worked with experimental microelectronics in conjunction with research efforts of department faculty. Assisted lower-division students in electronics laboratory with development and testing of microprocessors, chips and probes. Prepared analyses of micron chips fabricated in the lab for inclusion in published report.

Electronics Repair, Self-employed. 1992-94.
Operated small business in electronics repair servicing of computers, video recorders and small electronic appliances.

RELEVANT COURSEWORK:
Ultrasonic and frequency control
Telemetry and guidance
Instrumentation and measurement
Industrial electronics applications
Systems, manufacturing and cybernetics

COLLEGE HONORS/ACTIVITIES:
President, Tau Beta Phi Honor Society
President, IEEE West Texas State University Student Chapter
Lab Technician of the Year Award, Department of Electrical Engineering
Founding member, On Board, computer programmers club at WTSU

OTHER WORK EXPERIENCE:
Counter Clerk, Denton Video Rental. 1990-92.
Cook, Bob's Big Boy Burgers. 1988-90.

REFERENCES ON REQUEST

RAY-DEAN BENNETT
15543 Framington Lane
Walnut Creek, California 94595
(415) 555-0928

PROFESSIONAL OBJECTIVE

Design engineering in robotics automation for manufacturing.

EDUCATION

BSME, Mechanical Engineering, California Institute of Technology, 1993
BSEE, Electrical Engineering, California Institute of Technology, 1992

EXPERIENCE/SKILLS

- Strong mechanical and electrical engineering background, with course and lab emphasis in robotics and production-related problem solving.

- Extra coursework in heat sensing, CAD/CAM design, electronic control systems, computer programming (COBOL, PASCAL, BASIC), and image-enhancing technology.

- Won regional mechanical engineering competition for design of robotics manufacturing station for production of small motor.

- Extensive knowledge of automotive mechanics and related machinery. Worked in family-owned automotive repair shop for 8 years, including complete engine rebuilding and overhaul.

- Experienced with use of personal computers for design, word processing, database management, and spreadsheet functions.

MEMBERSHIPS
Student chapter of the IEEE and IAME • Tau Kappa Epsilon Honor Society

EMPLOYMENT HISTORY

Bennett's Auto Experts, Engine Mechanic, 1984-1992

REFERENCES

Available upon request

Warren Owen Pierce
12 Boxwood Lane
Oakwood, Illinois 60335
(815) 555-2368

Job Objective	A professional position in engineering safety with a local government agency, with emphasis on fire protection.
Education	<u>Bachelor of Science in Chemical Engineering</u>, University of Illinois, Chicago, 1993. GPA 3.86. Minor: Fire Protection Engineering. Major coursework included structures chemistry, chemical engineering, fire protection engineering, thermodynamics, hydrology, and electromagnetics.
Experience	<u>Intern</u>, Oakwood Fire Department, Oakwood, Illinois, Summer 1993. Employed full-time as assistant to the fire chief. Underwent rigorous three-week training in fire fighting, prevention, and protection. Participated in site clearances and arson investigations. Proposed new procedures for responding to college dormitory fire alarms, which resulted in a 25% increase in response time. <u>Assistant Safety Technician</u>, University of Illinois Public Health and Safety Department, Fall 1992 to Winter 1993. Worked part-time providing on-site training in public health and safety issues. Worked with safety specialists in fire, electrical, chemical, and nuclear emergency preparedness. Trained in recognizing potential fire, health, and safety hazards. <u>Residential Adviser</u>, University of Illinois Student Housing Department, Fall 1991 to Spring 1992. Supervised residential hall wing that housed 75 students. Responsible for safety surveillance, counseling, and coordinating building maintenance.
References	Available upon request.

TERRANCE W. WICKSTROM
230 S.E. First Avenue
White Beach, Florida 33128
407/555-0036

SUMMARY OF QUALIFICATIONS

Certified Professional Engineer. Twelve years of experience in engineering plus extensive experience in the design and installation of subterranean pipe systems, including layout design, routing, and isometric drawings for pipe spooling. Engineering design experience includes equipment support structures, equipment, and pipe supports. Extensive field experience with both large industrial and civil projects.

EDUCATION AND TRAINING

Bachelor of Science Degree, Engineering, University of Florida, Tampa, 1989.
      Engineering Coursework: fluids, mechanics, stress analysis, hydrology, stress
      dynamics, thermodynamics, water treatment engineering.

Associate of Science Degree, Engineering Specialty, College of Technology, Miami, 1981.
      Completed Engineering Technician training.

EMPLOYMENT HISTORY

Savenant & Ward, Construction Engineering
One S.W. Vermilion, Tampa, Florida
1986 to 1993
      Responsible for checking piping systems for proper construction against piping
      specifications and contact drawings. Checked fitting, welding, material class, and
      support structures. Conducted hydro testing of the systems and bolt torquing,
      according to specifications. Worked on the Shell Oil Company off-shore drilling
      project initial design phase.

J.L. Winterman and Associates, AIA, Architecture
126 Minter Avenue, Tampa, Florida
1981 to 1986
      Served as engineering technician on large-scale building designs for residential,
      commercial, industrial, and civil projects. Worked closely with structural engineers
      and city planners to design optimum installation plans for water and sewage pipe
      placement, routing, and support. Designed more efficient pipe support systems, now
      considered standard for multi-story structures in the Tampa area.

MEMBERSHIPS

National Society of Professional Engineers (NSPE)
Florida Society of Professional Engineers (FSPE)

REFERENCES ON REQUEST

Martie Johnson

P.O. Box 17384, Salt Lake City, UT 84132 / 801-555-2757

Objective

A position as field engineer with a large Northwest utility company, involving expertise in quality assurance, safety, and inspection.

Experience

Bechtel Power Corporation, Salt Lake City / January 1991 to present.

Field Engineer: Perform quality assurance inspections to comply with ASME codes in the installation of embedded and exposed piping of large diameter, sizing of structural components for supports, and checking of structural drawings and specifications.

Western Power Corporation, Salt Lake City / May 1985 to December 1990.

Designer and Field Engineer: Designed oil refinery piping systems. Inspected construction site and tested for stress, hydrology, and support. Performed stress analysis on plates, bolts, and structural steel.

Sundance International Corp., Salt Lake City / June 1980 to May 1985.

Designer and Checker: Checked design drawings for dimensional correctness, pipe size. Rendered layout and elevation drawings for construction projects. Provided on-site checking of "as built" drawings.

Mid-State Kiln Inc., Salt Lake City / June 1978 to June 1980.

Checker: Involved with checking equipment drawings for dimensional correctness and to determine the feasibility of constructing equipment as designed.

Education

A.E., 1974, Utah College of Technology, Salt Lake City.

U.S. Air Force, 1974 to 1978, Engineering crew of aircraft carrier, two years.

References

Provided upon request.

JOAN D. WILHITE
445 S. ALAMEDA • FLAGSTAFF, AZ 86024 • 602/555-3476

PROFESSIONAL OBJECTIVE
Chemical engineering position with supervisory and quality control responsibilities.

PROFESSIONAL EXPERIENCE

GEOTECHNICAL SPECIALTIES, INC., FLAGSTAFF, AZ

<u>Production Engineering Coordinator</u> (1992-Present)
- Monitoring production and controlling quality
- Troubleshooting production problems
- Supervising, training and motivating 21 technicians
- Daily production and downtime reports using MS Windows
- Working with chief engineers on production problem resolution
- Leading meetings, reviewing production and safety data
- Using Quality Analyst 4.2, producing capability studies and control charts
- Interacting with Accounting, Quality Control and Personnel on maximization of production line operation
- Best-running production line in the facility (out of 5)

<u>Engineering Technician</u> [Technical Services] (1990-1992)
- Chemical analysis on finished product (moisture analysis with Technicon/vacuum ovens; sodium analysis with atomic absorption using Perkin Elmer 3100; and ph/salt/titratable acidity)
- Finished product surveys and sensory evaluations
- Maintaining process data on Quality Analyst 4.2
- Assisting production coordinators on quality parameters to reduce potential problems
- Quality holds and re-auditing
- Setting up statistical sampling plans for held product
- Training management and union representatives on Statistical Methods for Improving Performance

NEWVISION INDUSTRIES, INC., PHOENIX, AZ

<u>Quality Assurance Chemist</u> (1988-1990)
- Analyzing raw ingredients/finished products/environmental swabs
- Conducting Good Manufacturing Practices (GMP) inspections and suggesting corrective measures where necessary
- Interacting with Sanitation Foreman on updating and implementing standardized cleaning procedures
- Writing/revising procedures manual
- Ordering Micro Laboratory supplies
- Increased volume of testing which resulted in improved troubleshooting and problem resolution

EDUCATIONAL BACKGROUND

B.S. Degree in Chemical Engineering (March 1988)
University of Washington, Seattle, WA

Continuing Education Seminars:
How to Organize & Manage Priorities (National Seminars Group)
Applications in the Management of Quality (Arizona Institute of Technology)
Certified Quality Technician [#7484] (American Society for Quality Control)
Statistical Methods for Improving Performance (Nabisco Food Groups)
Applied Statistical Quality Control Seminar (Northwest Analytical, Inc.)
Cultivating Supervisory Skills (Portland Community College)
Successful Communications Skills (Fred Pryor Seminar)
How to Work with Difficult People (National Seminars Group)

ACTIVITIES / MEMBERSHIPS

American Society of Quality Control (Arizona Chapter 1043)
American Society of Chemical Engineers (Arizona/University of Washington chapters)
Presented paper on pilot plant processing at ASCE conference, 1991, Washington, D.C.

References available upon request.

SARALYNNE KVITKA
654 SW Marshall St.
Jackson, Mississippi 39215
(601) 555-4932

EDUCATION:
Bachelor of Architecture, with a minor in Environmental Studies. University of
    Mississippi, March 1993.
    Areas of Emphasis:
    Structures, Geology, Geography
    Environmental Control Systems
    Public Planning, Policy, and Management
AutoCAD Levels I, II, and III, AutoDesk Training Center, Jackson Community
    College, certified August 1993.

EXPERIENCE:
Engineering Specialist
State of Mississippi, Engineering Division, Jackson (April 1993-present)
    Proofread, compiled, and distributed specifications. Designed files for drawing
    storage and organized current system. Conducted drawing research for various
    projects. Created database files for several Port accounts.

Engineering Intern
State of Mississippi, Engineering Division, Jackson (June 1992-Sept. 1992, Dec.
1992)
    Prepared and submitted permit applications. Received, processed, and
    distributed requests for utility locales. Updated house addressing maps for all
    facilities. Organized microfilm for all drawings from 1891 to 1985.

Draftsperson
Smithson, Davis & Forbes, Architects, Jackson (Jan. 1992-March 1992)
    Drafted preliminary through construction drawings. Researched building codes
    and product information. Practicum experience for academic credit.

Customer Service and Cashier
Howell's Supply Store, University, Mississippi (Sept. 1989-March 1993)
    Served 500 to 750 customers daily. Solitary employee in Art & Architecture
    Supply Store on weekends. Advised customers about product usage and brand
    comparison. Handled returns, exchanges, and personal/business charge
    accounts.

ADDITIONAL SKILLS:
Intermediate skills and experience with IBM software, including: AutoCAD,
Paradox, MS DOS, MS Windows 3.0-3.1, MS Word, WordPerfect, Excel, and
Lotus 1-2-3.
Some Macintosh experience including MS Word.
Art Media, Model Making, and Photography.

REFERENCES:
Available on request.

DAVON X. DESOTO
22 NE 56th Street
Pittsburgh, PA 15244
412-555-3742

OBJECTIVE

A supervisory/management position with an engineering firm that will challenge and enhance my experience, knowledge, skills and years of increasing responsibility.

HIGHLIGHTS OF QUALIFICATIONS

Twenty-three years of engineering, management and supervisory experience in managing facilities, equipment and personnel. Supervision of over 100 personnel. Extensive skills in planning, coordinating and supervising of projects. Reliable and adaptable; learn new systems quickly, and take initiative. Able to represent company with a professional appearance and manner.

WORK EXPERIENCE

Operation Supervisor, Suver Pennsylvania Compost Company, Inc.
1980-present.
Controlled entire plant operations of a 600 ton-per-day MSW facility with 100 employees. Assumed full responsibilities in absence of plant manager. Responsible for interviewing and hiring of employees, work schedules, daily production and technical inspections of equipment. Fully involved in daily performance testing. Provided training to all personnel.

Superintendent, Suver Waste Systems, Kingley Fast Disposal.
1976-1980.
Assumed responsibility of closure of KFD Landfill. Coordinated employee work schedules for ten personnel; truck delivery of closure material; work schedules of subcontractors tasked with installation of PVC liner. Economically solved soil erosion problems. Scheduled maintenance for and operated heavy equipment. Made purchases as needed for daily operations.

Group Engineer, Commissioned Chief Warrant Officer, USCG.
1972-1976.
Responsible for the direction of all civil and naval engineering support. Direct and indirect supervision of over 100 personnel for the maintenance of large patrol boats, small boats, Coast Guard facilities, including various duty stations and 97 housing units. Responsible for personnel training and budget management and procurement for a department with a budget of $250,000 annually and individual contracts in excess of $80,000. Other assigned duties included Safety Officer, Hazardous Waste Officer and Energy Conservation Coordinator.

Group Engineer, Senior Chief Machinery Technician, USCG.
1970-1972.
Responsible for the management and maintenance of two Coast Guard stations, two large patrol boats and several small boats, including electrical, propulsion and hydraulic systems. Responsible for development of computerized maintenance project list, budget administration and supervision of over 50 personnel.

DeSoto, 2

EDUCATION

Hazardous Waste Management, Leadership and Management, Procurement and Contraction, Oil Pollution and Law Enforcement, Collateral Duty Safety Officer, FBI Self Defense and Arrest Procedures, Emergency Medical Technician, First Aid and Personal Protection.

Western Missouri State College, General Studies. Sept. 1967-June 1969.

REFERENCES

Furnished immediately on request.

RASHAD AHMED
1287 NW Vine Ave., Jonesboro, Arkansas 72403 / 501/555-9846

OBJECTIVE

To work with a major engineering specialty firm in the development of new start-up enterprises.

PROFESSIONAL EXPERIENCE

January 1991 to present
VARITECH
Jonesboro, Arkansas
Position: Director

Developed a new business which includes managing the engineering, development, design, production, and marketing of a new product in the field of personal protection for women. The product was tremendously successful and marketed internationally.

February 1987 to December 1991
TURBOMAG CORPORATION
Dallas, Texas
Position: Director

Secured funds for venture capital from private sources in order to initiate the start of an energy research firm under the direction of the Technical Education Department (TED Center), Ft. Worth Community College. Upon receipt of the initial funds, I developed and managed the project as director and engineer. I was responsible for effective time and financial management, clear and precise project direction, research coordination, experimental results, consultant activity, machine shop fabrication, and working models.

July 1983 to February 1987
SOUTHWEST PIPELINE CORPORATION
Jonesboro, Arkansas
Position: Project contractor

Developed property and sub-divisions and remodeled homes as a sideline, including land clearing, street construction, building, and utility installation as contractor. Emphasis on utility and road construction.

EDUCATION

Edison Technical Institute
Dallas, Texas
B.S. Electrical Engineering 1983

Automation Institute
Little Rock, Arkansas
Electrical Engineering Technology Certificate 1990

AARON WILSON
224 Jubilee Road
Laramie, WY 82057
(307) 555-2753

SUMMARY

Seeking engineering technology position with company actively involved in geological structures and analysis. Engineering background. Excellent skills in problem solving, analytical thinking, and client relations. Self sufficient, industrious, organized, and work well with others.

EDUCATION

B.S. in Geology, California State University, Chico, CA, 1983.

Pursued additional course work in engineering at California Polytechnic University, San Luis Obispo, CA, 1980. Completed 60% of degree requirements.

Geology Courses

Geologic Mapping
Geology Field Camp
Structural Geology
Sedimentary Petrology
Igneous Petrology
Metamorphic Petrology
Geochemistry
Optical Crystallography
X-Ray Crystallography

Engineering Courses

Engineering Materials
Engineering Physics I, II, III
Metallurgical Engineering I
Thermodynamics I
Chemistry I, II, III
Calculus I, II, III
Linear Algebra

EXPERIENCE

Winston Laboratories, Ltd., Piedmont, TX, *Core Analyst,* 1991-1993.

Retrieved, catalogued, and preserved orientation of cores from oil fields and Superfund site. Represented company in the field. Described lithologies on site and in lab. Prepared samples of core by slabbing, photographing, selecting sample location, and plugging. Measured porosity, permeability, oil saturation, and gamma log response. Laid out core and discussed analysis with clients.

Fremont Construction, Inc., Hayward, CA, *Framing Foreman,* 1983-1990.

Built, remodeled, and restored large, custom homes in old, exclusive neighborhood for contracting firm. Experienced in all phases of construction. Prepared layout from architects' plans. Framed houses from foundation to roof. Supervised assistant carpenters and laborers. Coordinated subcontractors. Maintained client relationships and informed clients of progress.

References will be provided upon request.

CHEN WA CHANG
22 S. Gordon Ave.
Dallas, Texas 75232
214/555-4459

MAJOR EMPLOYMENT AND ACCOMPLISHMENTS

March 1987 to present
ITT COMMUNICATIONS
Houston, Texas
Position: District Manager

Served as manager responsible for the nine area counties for engineering and service. Prepared a budget and sales forecast for the service shop and sales staff; directed support and overhead costs, revenue projections, personnel management, sales and service programs, public relations and mountain top site development and management; employed the pinpoint marketing technique I developed at CBG Electronics.

September 1982 to February 1987
CBG ELECTRONICS DIVISION
Dallas, Texas
Position: Service Manager/Marketing Manager

Responsible for management of servicing and maintenance, mountain top site development, frequency coordination, customer relations for system changes and marketing. As marketing manager, designed a pinpoint marketing approach to sales efforts based on a study of market trends and license application histories that proved extremely effective; promoted this practice within the firm's sales and service personnel.

July 1975 to August 1978
SOUTHWEST COMMUNICATIONS
Dallas/Ft. Worth/Houston, Texas
Position: Sales Engineer

Managed sales activity for Southwest as well as regional manufacturer representative for organizations and service shops around twelve southwest and south-central states. Served as sales engineer, designing and promoting radiotelephone systems to all types of business and governmental agencies, i.e., rural fire and police protection agencies. Responsible for developing several mountain top communication sites, power transmission lines, tower design and construction, access roads, pipelines, and generator facilities.

September 1972 to June 1975
SEEDS, Inc.,
Dallas, Texas.
Position: Legislative Liaison

Responsible for lobbying, addressing and monitoring all proposed legislation for startup seed money for small businesses as part of the State Economic Development bill.

Chen Wa Chang
Page 2

EDUCATION

Southern Methodist University, Dallas, Texas.
Ph.D. - Applied Electronics, 1982.
Additional course work in business administration and marketing.

Southern Methodist University, Dallas, Texas.
B.S. - Communications Engineering, 1972.

MILITARY SERVICE

U.S. ARMY CORPS OF ENGINEERS, 1966-1969 Instructor: heavy equipment
operation, maintenance and safety.

PROFESSIONAL ORGANIZATIONS

Institute of Electrical and Electronic Engineers
American Physical Society
Society for Technical Communication

EXTENDED EDUCATION

"Sales Motivation" - ITT, Reno, Nevada.
"Sales Management" - ITT, Lynchburg, Virginia.
"Motivating People" - ITT, Portland, Oregon.
"Time Management" - ITT, Miami, Florida.
"Working With Government" - Southwestern Region Conference, IEEE, Phoenix,
Arizona.
"Business Planning" - Pryor Seminars, Dallas, Texas.
"Technical Writing" - Southwestern Region Conference, IEEE, Dallas, Texas.

REFERENCES

Available upon request.

Gregory G. Gaines
P.O. Box 234
Saginaw, MI 48603
(517) 555-4438

Experience Summary

More than seven years of varied hydrogeologic experience in performing and managing remedial investigations and assessments. Project responsibilities include design, implementation, and management of site investigation programs and personnel, subcontractor coordination, budget tracking, report preparation, and interaction with regulatory agencies.

Education

M.S. Geology, Oregon State University, Corvallis, OR, 1980.
    With strong emphasis in engineering technology.
B.A. Geology, Shawnee State University, Portsmouth, OH, 1978.

Work History

◊ Senior Engineer, Schmidt-Havens Engineering Corporation, Saginaw, MI.
  July 1988 to present. (Previous positions held include: Engineer, Senior Geologist, Engineering Specialist; 1980 to 1988.)

  Key projects include:
  ◊ Field team leader in charge of a remedial investigation (RI) at an NPL Superfund site in Detroit, MI. Responsible for implementing and managing the following field programs: surface water/sediment sampling, soil sampling, drilling, groundwater sampling, packer tests, air sampling, and residential well sampling. Also responsible for RI report.

  ◊ Field team leader in charge of drilling and monitoring of well installation at various sites for the Michigan Department of Transportation.

  ◊ Supervised drilling and monitoring of well installation at various oil and gas terminals and service stations throughout northern Michigan as part of a property transfer.

  ◊ Supervised a soil boring and sampling program at a Minnesota rubber manufacturing facility. Responsible for field investigation reports.

  ◊ Supervised a hydrogeologic investigation, including drilling, monitoring well installation, soil and groundwater sampling, at a major steel manufacturing facility in Pennsylvania. Responsible for field investigation reports.

Professional Affiliations

AIPG Certified Professional Geologist
Registered Professional Geologist, Michigan, Minnesota, Pennsylvania, Ohio,
   Indiana, Illinois, Iowa, New York
Certified Engineering Technician
Member, Association of Groundwater Scientists and Engineers

References

Provided upon request. Registration numbers and certificates also available.

Charles Andawa

4783 West Maple • Baltimore, Maryland 21233 • 301 555-2983

Objective: A position in Chemical Engineering with a Federal Agency

Experience:

1978-present Senior Project Manager, PPD, Inc., Baltimore, MD

Report to Senior Vice President of Engineering. Supervise thirty-two employees. Direct, supervise, administer, and manage several projects from inception to start-up, including new chemical process equipment manufacturing. Assist Sales Department in reviewing the system process design, scheduling, engineering, and costs before final proposal is presented to client.

Conceived, initiated, and developed chemical formations for non-toxic solutions for use in oil recovery and recycling. Formulated empirical equations and design criteria for the system, which resulted in increasing company sales seven-fold over the last five years.

Instituted procedures for project document handling, filing, and project communication, including project status summaries to management and clients.

Trained project engineers and project managers to design and manage projects.

Participated in developing service-system study concept to introduce PPD's name into new markets, which increased sales by fifty percent in that market.

1974-1978 Senior Project and Process Engineer, Moreland Chemical, Annapolis, MD

Project experience included Pulp Liquor Evaporation System operations, sand reclamation systems, waste wood utilization to manufacture charcoal, sewage sludge oxidation, waste oxidation, and heat recovery. Responsible for planning, scheduling, process design, and specifications.

Held complete process and project responsibility of four projects from proposal stage through plant start-up, including budgeting. Supervised twenty-three chemical and physical engineers and laboratory technicians.

1972-1974 Process and Plant Engineer, Cecero's, Inc., Annapolis, MD

Major responsibilities included chemical plant trouble-shooting, process studies, process development, project cost estimation, equipment design, equipment sizing, selection, and purchasing, utility optimization, air and water pollution controls, boiler and incinerator operations, and coordination of plant work with production department.

1969-1972 Process Development Engineer, U.S. Chemical Co., Philadelphia, PA

Worked on a solvent exchange and through-air drying of tissue paper. Operated the high speed pacer machine to test the through-air drying concept.

Education:

M.S. Chemical Engineering, Minnesota Technical University, Houghton, MN, 1969

References available by request

JEFFERSON BIRD
3829 HIGH ROAD
WARWICK, RI 02887
401 555-9287

OBJECTIVE
A POSITION IN ENGINEERING MANAGEMENT IN THE PUBLIC SECTOR

BACKGROUND SUMMARY
Over twenty years experience in construction and mechanical engineering for private corporations, specifically: field engineer for installation of propulsion turbine plant on land-based test site; industrial and product engineering in the shipbuilding, material handling, chemical, and gas industries in construction, maintenance, engineering, and administrative capacities.

EDUCATION
M.S., Mechanical Engineering, 1969, Eastern University, Springfield, MA

B.S., Mechanical Engineering, 1965, Pennsylvania Institute of Technology, Pittsburgh, PA

EXPERIENCE
1982-1992

Newport Shipbuilders, Inc., Warwick, RI
Senior Engineer

- Supported construction and operating personnel during installation, start-up, and testing of propulsion, generator, and hydraulic machinery.
- Performed facility survey, prepared technical reports, and provided engineering support during construction, start-up, and testing of the propulsion turbine plant.
- Assisted in construction during structural and mechanical equipment support and foundation.
- Coordinated fabrication and installation of full size mock-up for integrated sub-base turbo generator.
- Provided support to designers, draftsmen, and construction personnel to ensure compliance with technical specifications and code requirements.

1974-1982

Shipbuilders Corporation, Providence, RI
Engineering Supervisor

- Designed various mechanical and fluid systems and assisted in procurement, installation, and testing of systems and equipment.
- Designed and assisted in construction and testing of a flow-through crude oil handling system on 120,000 ton double-hull tanker, reducing initial cost and increasing operational efficiency.
- Organized a multi-disciplinary team to develop and build an oil-water separator to meet pollution control requirements.
- Conducted equipment and system test at the factory and after completion of installation for various components, including pumps, heat exchangers, hydraulics, and control/monitoring devices.
- Assisted in installation and testing of bulk petrochemical heating system to maintain the product temperature.

1969-1973   **TEC, Fiber Division**, Boston, MA
Staff Engineer

- Assisted during installation, start-up, and testing of machinery for fiber, film cellulose, and bulk material and processing equipment.
- Developed and assisted in installation of automated overhead conveying system to replace manual material handling operation for cellulose sheet.
- Supervised installation of the filling line to increase bagging output for micro crystalline cellulose.
- Redesigned the PVC blown film machine and provided assistance during installation and start-up.

1965-1967   **Pennsylvania Oxygen Corp., Ltd.**, Pittsburgh, PA
Assistant Engineer

- Supervised a work force of 120 with responsibility over production and maintenance of oxygen and acetylene plant and facilities.
- Conducted the economic analysis for relocating oxygen plant. Supervised erection of the plant at the new site.
- Designed and assisted in the fabrication of the filtering system for acetylene. Supervised start-up and the testing of the system.
- Developed the test procedure for high pressure cylinders to meet regulatory requirements.

REFERENCES ON REQUEST

Donna Everson
1233 Mission Street
San Pablo, California 98329
212/555-0812

Goal	An engineering management position requiring analysis and strategic planning.
Education	Massachusetts Institute of Technology, 1974 MS, Civil Engineering
	University of California, Los Angeles, 1972 BS, Engineering
Experience	CH2M Hill, Inc. 1985 - present **Civil Engineer**

- Responsible for analysis and design of transportation systems.

- Coordinated planning and construction with city, state, and federal government engineers.

- Successfully negotiated contract for $26.8 million in highway construction for the city of Los Angeles.

- Responsible for developing cost-benefit ratios, staff and material estimates and schedules, and project budgets.

- Experienced with computer-aided design, drafting, and structural analysis.

Shell Oil Company
1975 - 1984
Engineering Sales Specialist

- Responsible for home heating oil sales program and technical support for distribution companies.

- Designed and implemented a marketing program for potential distributors that resulted in 23% increased sales over the previous year.

- Developed a network of technical support for both distributors and end-users of the product.

- Coordinated marketing and sales programs with heater manufacturers to stimulate sales in the small business market.

- Provided technical support to manufacturers and distributors for selecting appropriate weight and type of oil according to burner specifications.

Honors	Michaelson-Davis Award for Outstanding Contribution from a New Employee, 1986 Who's Who in Engineering, 1990 Chapter President, Society of Women Engineers, 1989 - 1991 Phi Kappa Phi Delta Upsilon Pi, Engineering Honorary
References	Available on request

KEVIN FOXWORTH
2114 Renton Street
Kirkland, Washington 98005
206/555-3497

CAREER OBJECTIVE — Engineering position with industrial manufacturing company.

EDUCATION

| 1988 | BS, Engineering, University of Washington |
| 1963 | AA, Technology & Industry Production, Everett Community College, Everett, Washington |

CAPABILITIES

- Manage continuous fire furnaces that produce flat pressed glass and glass for machine and hand blowing.

- Plan and supervise all aspects of furnace operation and maintenance, including personnel scheduling and staffing.

- Evaluate alternative production methods and materials to reduce costs and improve product quality.

- Control raw materials inventory, ordering, and inspection.

- Train employees in use and maintenance of equipment.

- Review product availability and equipment developments to keep systems up-to-date for both production and safety concerns.

- Plan, coordinate, and supervise all aspects of glassware production.

ACHIEVEMENTS

- Initiated improved method for raw materials handling that resulted in $250,000 in actual savings.

- Worked with production engineers to develop new heating procedures that made furnaces 20 percent more efficient in start-up time.

- Developed operating procedures that improved worker safety.

- Designed alternative casing that reduced external temperatures dramatically, thus decreasing fire and burn hazard.

- Given Award of Merit for developing material composition that produced greater clarity in pressed glass products.

WORK HISTORY

| 1975 - present | Pilchuck GlassWorks Factory, Seattle, Washington
Furnace/Production Manager |
| 1964 - 1975 | Boeing, Renton, Washington
Senior Technician, Instrumentation Casing Section |

REFERENCES — Available when requested.

Stephen Monetti
34 South Avon Street
Charleston, South Carolina 29411
603.555-2236

Career Objective

Senior Engineer leading to Project Director position

Career Achievements

Direct, supervise, and administer turn-key projects from inception to start-up for equipment manufacturing firm.

Coordinate with sales department to review system process design, equipment sizes, schedule, and engineering costs before presenting final proposal to the client.

Negotiate purchases and advise corporate president and CEO of pending contracts and negotiations.

Completed seventeen domestic projects and twenty international projects in Latin America, South America, Spain, and Africa.

Conceived, initiated, and successfully sold design of two new equipment products that resulted in a 40 percent increase in corporate sales over two years.

Completed all projects on or ahead of schedule. All projects resulted in corporate profits; many produced higher profits than anticipated.

Instituted procedures for project document handling and project communication.

Trained project engineers and project managers to design and manage assigned projects.

Instituted program for college interns and developed training program that culminated in job offers to those graduates whose performance met challenges of the position. After seven years, all students thus hired are still with the company and highly productive.

Supervise four project management teams, including twelve engineers and sixteen draftsmen.

Acted as site project engineer during construction of $250 million plant.

Registered professional engineer in the states of South Carolina and Arkansas.

Career Experience

Senior Engineer, DRG Inc., Charleston, South Carolina, 1978-present
Senior Project and Process Engineer, Hopewell Systems, Charleston, 1974-78
Process and Plant Engineer, Wembley Haddon, Inc., Little Rock, Arkansas, 1972-74
Consultant Engineer, Toverston Dryers, Little Rock, 1971-72
Pilot Plant and Process Development Engineer, James River Corp., Neenah, Wisconsin, 1967-71

Education

M.S. Chemical Engineering, Georgia Institute of Technology, Atlanta, 1978
B.S. Engineering, University of Wisconsin, Milwaukee, 1967

Professional References Available as Requested

Darius G.W. Harms
3485 Plainfield Road
Lincoln, Nebraska 68573
402-555-9287

Career Goal	A POSITION IN ENGINEERING MANAGEMENT IN THE PUBLIC SECTOR
Achievements & **Experience**	

- Supported construction and operating personnel during installation, start-up, and testing of propulsion generator and hydraulic machinery.
- Performed facility survey, prepared technical reports, and provided engineering support during construction, start-up, and testing of the propulsion turbine plant.
- Directed structural and mechanical equipment development and operations.
- Coordinated fabrication and installation of full-size mock-up for integrated sub-base turbo generator.
- Provided support to designers, draftsmen, and construction personnel to ensure compliance with technical specifications and code requirements.
- Designed various mechanical and fluid systems and assisted in procurement, installation, and testing of systems and equipment.
- Designed and assisted in construction and testing of a flow-through crude oil handling system on oil recycler, reducing initial cost and increasing operational efficiency.
- Conducted equipment and system test at the factory and after site installation of various recycling components, including pumps, heat exchangers, hydraulics, and control/monitoring devices.
- Assisted in installation and testing of bulk petrochemical heating system.
- Assisted during installation, start-up, and testing of machinery for fiber, film cellulose, bulk material, and processing equipment.
- Developed and assisted in installation of automated overhead conveying system to replace manual material handling operation for cellulose sheet.
- Supervised installation of the filling line to increase bagging output for micro crystalline cellulose.
- Redesigned the PVC blown film machine and provided assistance during installation and start-up. Supervised a work force of 120 with responsibility over production and maintenance of oxygen and acetylene plant and facilities.
- Conducted the economic analysis for relocating oxygen plant. Supervised erection of the plant at the new site.
- Designed and assisted in the fabrication of the filtering system for acetylene. Supervised start-up and the testing of the system.
- Developed the test procedure for high pressure cylinders to meet regulatory requirements.

Work History

1988-1993	**Benton Recycling Machinery, Inc.**, Lincoln, Nebraska *Senior Engineer*
1979-1988	**Taber Manufacturing**, Lincoln, Nebraska *Engineering Supervisor*
1965-1979	**Tutwiller Bond Oxygen Corp., Ltd.**, Topeka, Kansas *Staff Engineer, Maintenance Engineer, Technician*

Education   M.S., Mechanical Engineering, 1971, University of Kansas
B.S., Mechanical Engineering, 1965, University of Nebraska-Lincoln

References on request

Serena Pederson

334 Beca Street
Reno, NV 89564
(702) 555-0227

Career Goal

Seeking employment as an associate engineer or mechanical drafter with the engineering department of a major civil engineering firm that offers opportunities for challenge and advancement.

Experience and Work History

2/92 to present
Calham Engineering
West Bonnaville, Nevada

Mechanical Drafter - Mechanical drafting and layout of commercial piping, construction, and on-site sketch drawings of general mechanical layouts.

11/90 to 2/92
Interstate Engineering Company
Las Vegas, Nevada

Mechanical Drafter - Mechanical drafting and layout of marine piping, drawings and electrical diagrams, and on site sketch drawings of piping and electrical. As-built floor plan drawings.

1/89 to 11/90
Northwest Cedar Homes/Lindal Cedar Homes
Seattle, Washington

Architectural Drafter - Drafting and design of presentation floor plans and elevation site plans in accordance to company and client specifications. Consulting with clients on custom home designs and site plans. Delivery of building materials to job sites.

Education

B.S. Civil Engineering, University of Nevada-Las Vegas, 1993
GPA: 3.5

Extensive classes in architectural drafting from Portland Community
College, Portland, OR, including:

Residential Design
Structural Design
Piping and Electrical Design
Auto Cad
Building Codes

Associate of Applied Sciences Degree (Criminal Justice),Portland
Community College, Portland, OR, 1986

Activities and Hobbies

Drawing, painting, tennis and racquetball, gardening.

References

ROGER W. FENTON
223 S. Cameron Drive
St. Paul, MN 55223
(612) 555-0443

SUMMARY OF QUALIFICATIONS

Achievement-oriented leader, team player, dedicated to "continuous improvement."
Diverse experience, including engineering, manufacturing, quality control, customer
service, distribution, management, and supervision. Areas of major emphasis include
employee and labor relations (extensive background managing in a union shop),
machining and assembly, hot extrusion, injection molding, electro-plating, safety,
budget and forecasting, absentee control, training, and training management.

WORK EXPERIENCE

PLASTIMADE Corp., St. Paul, MN   1993 - Present
(Manufacturer of vinyl products for industrial, government, and consumer markets.)

PRODUCTION MANAGER
Manage 31 employees in all phases of manufacturing, distribution, quality, inventory,
and maintenance operations. Hire, fire, review, and provide all other personnel
actions. Turned around a troubled manufacturing operation with severe quality and
productivity deficiencies, in time to support high demand season sales. Eliminated the
most costly quality defect - reduced warranty returns to zero.

Increased production 220%. Increased average individual productivity by 14%.
Ensured a safe working environment, with no lost time accidents.

STANLEY INDUSTRIAL TOOLS, Milwaukee, WI   1980 - 93
(Manufacturer of mechanics' hand tools, including sockets and torque wrenches.)

PRODUCTION SUPERVISOR
Managed multiple departments, supervised up to 78 employees, responsible for 3
shifts and continuous operations. Planned product, equipment, and manpower to
meet production requirements. Requisitioned and maintained inventories of tooling
and operating supplies. Developed and controlled multi-million-dollar department
budgets; prepared expense forecasts. Maintained a safe, positive, and productive work
environment.

Utilized group technology principles to achieve "zero cost" labor operations. Reduced
product lead times by 5 weeks, inventory by 20%, and customer back-orders by 98%.
Managed 5 product improvement teams (quality circles), implementing modern
quality management techniques, i.e., SPC and ISO 9002 international quality
standards. Realized more than $200,000 in annual savings.

Developed and implemented "Safety Awareness" program achieving a lost-time rate
45% below the national industry average. Developed manufacturing process for 29
models of "industry's best" torque wrenches. Modified electro-plating system,

achieving a 36% reduction in process time, a 20% reduction in rework, and doubled operational efficiency. Managed national product repair center; reduced repair time 63%. Developed operator training programs and setup procedures for key equipment.

STANLEY INDUSTRIAL TOOLS, Wichita Falls, TX   1978 - 80

MANUFACTURING ENGINEER
Managed start-up operations for the manufacture of torque wrench components. Developed and implemented machining methods; established product costs. Prepared manufacturing plans and process prints. Designed fixtures and specified tooling. Implemented vendor and in-house manufacturing for 387 components, decreasing lead times by 64 days. Established a quality program to support manufacturing, reducing scrap and rework by 87%.

STANLEY INDUSTRIAL TOOLS, Denver, CO   1974 - 78

FOREMAN
Successfully transferred the torque wrench product line to the Colorado plant; increased annual shipments by $4 million dollars. Specified and procured "state of the art" calibration equipment with an accuracy 2.5 times greater than the competitors. Implemented two union wage reclassifications, yielding a labor savings of 11%. Designed assembly workstations and component storage area to complement each other; reduced material handling by 66%. Set up and managed component parts inventory valued over $1 million.

EDUCATION

BELLEVUE COMMUNITY COLLEGE, Bellevue, WA
A.S. Electronics Technology   1974
Geometric Dimensioning/Tolerancing CNC Lathe Programming
CNC Machine Tools (Programming) Heat Treatment of Materials Engineering Project Management

Additional Training:
Certificate in Supervisory Training
Dale Carnegie Management System
Statistical Process Control (SPC)
"Just in Time" (JIT) Inventory
Electro-plating and Finishing

JORJE S. HERNANDEZ
P.O. Box 4432 • Las Cruces, New Mexico 88011 • 505-555-0375

OBJECTIVE	Pursue a career track in environmental engineering with a large private or public agency.

WORK EXPERIENCE

08/90-present	Environmental Engineer Brigante & Solo, Inc. Las Cruces, New Mexico Prepare environmental assessments and checklists, noise level predictions, ambient noise levels. Advise design engineering on environmental problems, design cross sections, estimate construction quantities. Compute wetland involvement.
07/88-08/90	Utilities Relocation Engineer Arizona State Department of Transportation Phoenix, Arizona Work with public utilities in relocation of facilities within public right of way. Coordinate movement and develop movement agreements. Enforce clear zone.
06/85-07/88	Engineer Arizona State Department of Transportation Phoenix, Arizona Coordinate, review, revise, and process U.S. Army Corps of Engineer permits, shorelines, flood plains, and hydraulic permits. Prepare environmental checklists, impact statements, noise level predictions, ambient noise levels, and air level pollution levels. Investigate and advise for hazardous material spills, underground storage tanks, and site assessments. Prepare displays for public and court meetings. Review environmental documents, permits, interpret noise levels on projects, design noise barrier, and monitor and collect air quality. Review and approve large lots, short plats, and roadway approaches for private developers. Assemble and calibrate nine air quality control sets valued at $175,000.00 each.
EDUCATION	B.S. Engineering, University of New Mexico, 3.8 GPA, High Honors. References will be provided on request.

GEENA MICKELSON
Professional Office Complex 2, Suite 34, Boise, Idaho 83732
(208) 555-3453 - FAX (208) 555-3476

General Qualifications

I have been a SEPA-NEPA engineer for over 13 years for Idaho State Department of Transportation projects. I was responsible for assessments, air quality, noise level surveys, permitting, and environmental projects. Conducted surveys and projected noise level surveys. Wrote major portions of the department's many environmental assessments, and 10,000 - 20,000 environmental checklists. Determined wetland involvement prior to 1987. Coordinated all State, Federal, and Local permits (according to NEPA and SEPA requirements), and coordinated and negotiated for mitigation. Investigated for hazardous waste occurrence.

For six years screened WSDOT district projects for archaeological and historical significance and contracted for evaluation services. Served as the coordinator for District Interdisciplinary Team.

Seven years experience as highway engineer for foundation investigation, route survey, geologically sensitive areas, resolved water source pollution, and correction and landslide investigation and correction.

Recent Work History

Senior Transportation Engineer - July 1987 to present
Idaho State Department of Transportation, Boise, Idaho

Inspector on construction projects for new roadways. Test samples and test for quality control. Coordinate contractor schedules. Served as survey party chief for two years.

Transportation Engineer - June 1980 to July 1987
Idaho State Department of Transportation, Boise, Idaho

Test soil samples prior to highway construction and foundation preparation. Make recommendations for quality control, sand equivalent, fine and course grade compaction, soil settlement, asphalt extraction, and soil and aggregate mix ratio.

Education & Training

University of Idaho - Bachelor of Science (Geology), 1971
University of Idaho - Secondary Certificate (Engineering) 1972
Engineering in the 90s Workshops - 1990, 1992
Effective Report Writing, WSDOT - 1983, 1984
Acoustic Seminar, WSDOT - 1980
Water Quality Research Workshop - U.W. 1983
Noise Highway Traffic and Fundamentals, FHWA - 1989
Teletype Operators Course, 4 months, 1983
Miscellaneous Basic Computer Courses, WSDOT - 1990
Underground Storage Tank Removal Certificate - 1990
80 Hour Hazardous Waste Handlers Certification, OSHA, EPA - 1989

References available on request.

JOHN B. HANAKA
665 W. Paloma Drive
Tempe, AZ 85275
602/555-4439

PROFESSIONAL AMBITION:

A career in mechanical engineering.

EDUCATION:

ARIZONA STATE UNIVERSITY, Tempe, AZ
MS 1993, Mechanical Engineering
BS 1980, Business, with minor in Industrial Design

QUALIFICATIONS IN BRIEF:

Master's degree in mechanical engineering. Graduated 12th in a class of 218. Ten years in materials management, operations and customer service. Ability to analyze and prepare budget forecasts, financial statements and analytical reports. Proficiency in IBM-36 mainframe and PC. Software applications include AutoCAD, Lotus, Excel, WordPerfect, Dbase IV, QuattroPro. Supervised, trained and coordinated group activities.

CONTRACT AND PART-TIME EMPLOYMENT:

MACHINE WORKS INDUSTRIES, Tempe, AZ
Purchasing Manager, Jan. - Nov., 1993

Developed and implemented JIT Materials Management Program for corporate offices and 13 warehouse outlets. Negotiated and purchased three-location, 400-extension telecommunication system. Responsible for $17 million in purchasing. Reported to Finance Director. Contracted to install JIT Materials Management Program. Contract ended at completion of project.

JOHNSON & JOHNSON, Tempe, AZ
Merchandiser, 1990 - 1992

Assisted field sales and helped coordinate and set up promotions in retail and trade shows. Part-time position used to finance education. Left in good standing.

PROFESSIONAL EXPERIENCE:

DESERT STATES FASTENING SYSTEMS; INC., Tempe, AZ
Buyer/Inventory Control Manager 1984 - 1991

Coordinated day to day warehouse operations. Supervised 12 employees. Managed inventory control levels and purchasing activities. $20-30 million sales revenue in the fastener industry. Reported to General Manager. Corporation relocated to Kent, Washington. My commitment to education necessitated the decline of employer's offer to move.

FLEXALLOY, INC., Flagstaff, AZ
Buyer/Warehouse Manager, 1980 - 1984

Developed and implemented JIT system reducing inventory levels by 20% and reducing freight costs by 50% while increasing operating efficiency. Reported to Vice President of Operations. Employer downsized; left in good standing.

REFERENCES available on request.

```
NAVRONE W. GRIFFITH
17 NE THIRD AVENUE
REEDSVILLE, PENNSYLVANIA 17084-3384
(814) 555-5089
```

CAREER GOAL

My career objective is to become an integral part of a
progressive, growth-oriented corporation in the areas of
engineering and management.

EDUCATION

1993 - B.S. Fluid Power Engineering, Milwaukee School of
    Engineering, Milwaukee, WI (Minor taken in Air Conditioning
    Engineering Technology)

Journeyman Plumber (PA)

Certification for teaching Heating and Air Conditioning (PA)

CAREER SUMMARY

CASE HOME HEATING AND PLUMBING
1/80 to 9/92 - Cincinnati, Ohio
Part-Owner, Manager, Journeyman Plumber

Responsible for generating business and assigning workers to
complete contracted projects for private, corporate, and civil
clients. Worked closely with engineering consultants on major
plumbing and heating installation projects for multi-story
buildings and large residential complexes. Became part-owner,
but sold interest to return to college to pursue an
engineering career.

MEMBERSHIPS

National Society of Black Engineers (President of student
    chapter at MSE)
American Society of Heating, Refrigeration and Air
    Conditioning Engineers, Inc.
American Water Resources Association

REFERENCES

Available on request.

PAULA R TREMONE
67 W. Tanner, No. 445
Concord, NH 03307
(603) 555-2940

OBJECTIVE:

A responsible position in structural engineering with a civil engineering firm.

SUMMARY OF QUALIFICATIONS:

- Bachelor's degree in structural engineering, graduating with honors.
- Extensive experience in design and construction of commercial and residential structures.
- Reviewed and recommended bids.
- Hired subcontractors.
- Provided on-site supervision of subcontractors.
- Supervised installation of sprinkler systems.
- Construction of offshore oil rigs, mobile home parks and recreation homes.
- Flat concrete work, electrical, plumbing, and framing.
- Read blueprints and drawings.

EXPERIENCE:

1987 - 1992	**TREMONE AND ASSOCIATES, INC.** Concord, NH **Co-Owner/Operator**

Responsible for the day-to-day operation of construction firm as well as consultant for Barker Engineering, Ltd., precision engineering brokers.

1985-1987	**BARKER ENGINEERING, LTD.** Concord, NH **Manager**

Manager of this precision engineering brokerage firm, responsible for hiring, firing, reviewing subcontractors' bids, and negotiating contracts.

1982 - 1985	**RAJ, INC.** Santa Cruz, CA **Superintendent**

Engaged in ground up construction, bank ATM installations, earthquake-proofing of older buildings, and structural steel. Also, general construction of custom homes, apartment buildings, restaurants, remodels, roads and parkways, a trailer and mobile home park.

EDUCATION:

1993	B.S. Structural Engineering, University of New Hampshire Durham, NH
1981	A.A.S. Construction Technology, UC Santa Cruz Santa Cruz, CA

MUHAMMAD SERAW
2121 W. Hampstead Ln.
Rutland, VT 05702

(802) 555-4312 (Days)
(802) 555-4375 (Fax)
(802) 555-3411 (Eves)

OBJECTIVE

Position in engineering management with the construction department of a large engineering consulting firm.

EMPLOYMENT

City of Rutland, Rutland, VT (1988-1993)
PUBLIC WORKS INSPECTOR II (8/92-3/93):
- Coordinated and performed public works inspections for compliance with project plans, standards, and specifications on projects up to $3 million.
- Ensured proper materials, methods, and procedures were utilized.
- Interpreted construction requirements for contractors/property owners and assisted in compliance.
- Conducted final inspections and submitted corrections as needed.
- Assisted project civil engineering preparation, revision, and execution of cost estimates, working drawings, change orders, and progress payments.
- Prepared all state and federal on-site records on daily basis.

ENGINEERING TECHNICIAN II (7/90-8/92):
- Coordinated permits and certificates of occupancy.
- Scheduled and coordinated preconstruction meetings with city staff contractors and developers, ensuring that all requirements and conditions for the development were met.
- Arranged engineering inspections and served as liaison between all relevant parties.
- Provided general and technical information concerning city codes, specifications, standards, deeds, easements, utilities, and improvement plans and other related information.
- Processed agreements, bonds, insurance certificates, and other financial provisions for developments.
- Researched and compiled data for monthly and annual reports for city departments and other governmental agencies.

Sullivan Construction, Waterford, CT (4/88-6/90)
ASSISTANT PROJECT MANAGER:
- Consistently came in under budget while responsible for all purchasing and hiring.
- Prepared material take-offs, subcontractor bid packages, purchased construction materials.
- Processed invoices for payment on $20 million multi-family, residential projects.
- Reviewed subcontractors' submissions for compliance with architect's and engineer's specifications.
- Reviewed and approved general and subcontractor's schedules, conducting weekly job-site meetings to eliminate contractor interference and arranging all local, state, and federal inspections.
- Supervised job-site superintendents, conducting initial field hiring of all general contractor's staff.

SERAW
Page 2

EMPLOYMENT HISTORY (continued)

• Cappers, Inc., Manchester, CT (10/82-4/88)
PURCHASING AGENT:
• Purchased construction materials for residential, commercial, and industrial projects of up to $10 million, achieving up to a 75% rate of under-budget purchases.
• Assisted in administration of several HUD housing complexes.
• Assembled subcontractor bid packages including receiving and recommended award of bid.
• Established apprenticeship programs with state trade organizations.

• CFD Construction, Inc., Greenwich, RI (5/80-10/82)
ASSISTANT SUPERINTENDENT:
• Scheduled material deliveries to sites.
• Prepared certified payrolls.
• Scheduled subcontractors, inspections, and assigned work to General Contractor's staff.

EDUCATION

B.S. Engineering & Construction Technology, University of Maine, Farmington, 1988.
A.A.S. Construction & Design, Fort Kent Community College, Maine, 1980.

References upon request.

JASON SWIFT
2216 Marshall Heights Road, Apt. G3
New Orleans, LA 70112
(504) 555-4450

CAREER OBJECTIVE

An entry-level position in Civil Engineering.

EDUCATION

<u>Oregon State University, Corvallis, OR.</u>

Specialization: Civil Engineering Professional School.

Degree: Bachelor of Science in Civil Engineering, 6/93.

Course work:
<u>Engineering:</u>
Statics, Dynamics, Strength of Materials, and Thermodynamics.

<u>Civil Engineering:</u>
Environmental Engineering, Fluid Mechanics, Materials, Soil Mechanics, Structural Design, Surveying, and Transportation.

<u>Southern Technical College, New Orleans, LA.</u>

Specialization: General education and pre-engineering.

Degree: Associate of Science, 12/90.

E.I.T. Certificate.

WORK EXPERIENCE

Landscape Subcontractor, Corvallis, OR, Summer 1990 and 1991.

Crew Member, Crowd Management Services, Corvallis, OR, Summer 1991 and 1992.

ACTIVITIES

Currently enrolled in certification course for AutoCAD Release 12.
National Member of the American Society of Civil Engineers.
A.S.C.E. student chapter Vice President.
A.S.C.E. student workshop.
American Institute of Steel Construction bridge design competition, 92-93.
Sports (baseball, swimming, waterpolo, basketball, and fishing).
Woodworking.

JOANNA CASSIDY
2287 S.W. 29th Place
Savannah, GA 31406
(912) 555-4986

OBJECTIVE
- Construction Management position with large engineering firm, utilizing my background and education in construction engineering technology and extensive managerial experience.

EDUCATION
- CONSTRUCTION MANAGEMENT: UCLA, Los Angeles, CA (1990-1992)
  B.S. Degree, 1992
- DESIGN AND CONSTRUCTION ENGINEERING: Austin Peay State College, Clarksville, TN (1986-1988)
  B.S. Degree, 1988
- CONSTRUCTION ENGINEERING TECHNOLOGY: Middlesex Community College, Middleton, CT (1983-1985)
  Certificate: 1985

QUALIFICATIONS
- Public works inspections
- Report preparation
- Expense control/reductions
- Operations/materials management

SKILLS
- Staff hiring/management
- Quality control
- Procurement operations
- Permit procedures

ACHIEVEMENTS
- Consistently brought in construction projects under budget.
- Achieved materials procurement rate up to 75% under budget.
- Instituted apprenticeship program in conjunction with state trade organizations.

CERTIFICATIONS
- PUBLIC WORKS INSPECTOR: UCLA, Los Angeles, CA (1991)
- CONCRETE FIELD TECHNICIAN: American Concrete Institute (1989)
- FITTER: General Dynamics, Electric Boat Division, Apprenticeship (1976)

CASSIDY - 2

EMPLOYMENT HISTORY
- Jones & Marks, Ltd., Architectural Engineering (Intern, Summer 1992; part-time, 1992-present)
  Hired part-time after serving three-month paid internship (selected from among 75 applicants), taking full advantage of on-the-job training in construction design and engineering. Responsible for maintaining blueprints, change notices, design meeting records. Worked with consulting engineers on site preparation, evaluation of design blueprints, and review of construction schedules.

- Design Assistant, Austin Peay State College, Clarksville, TN (1987-1988)
  Worked with faculty on work-for-hire projects from engineering firms and construction contractors. Prepared drawings, conducted stress management calculations, tested other analyses for accuracy.

COMMUNITY SERVICE
- Habitat for Humanity: solicited donations of materials and contractor's crews to build housing for low-income families; provided labor (1988-1993).
- Graffiti Abatement Coordinator: solicited donations of materials and coordinated volunteers (1993).
- St. Marks Homeless Shelter Holiday Drive: coordinated city staff volunteers (1992).

REFERENCES AVAILABLE UPON REQUEST

THOMAS CARTER
21 Interstate Street * Portland, Maine 04121 * (207) 555-4335

PROFESSIONAL GOALS

To develop an engineering career with a successful company in the area of machine design, gain a professional engineering certificate and continue my education.

PROFESSIONAL EXPERIENCE

Project Engineer/Engineering Manager - Sherwin-Williams Paint Co. - 8/88 to present
* Engineering duties include design conception, documentation and implementation as specified by customer. Act as liaison between engineering and sales departments, from bid to shipment.
* Achievements include introducing two new products into the Sherwin-Williams line.
* Managerial duties include setting engineering documentation policy, workload distribution and giving input on production schedule and plant operation.

Engineering Assistant - Debenham Mfg. - 6/87 to 9/87
* Duties included AutoCAD drafting and hands-on work with prototype machines in the research and development department.

Engineering Assistant - Portland Veterans Hospital - 3/83 to 9/84
* Duties included monitoring building HVAC system and metal fabrication.

EDUCATIONAL EXPERIENCE

BSME - Oregon State University - 6/88
* Achieved a GPA of 3.2/4.0 for classes taken in the professional program.
* Acted as Group leader for the Computer Controlled Walking Machine Senior Project.
* Elective course work included Finite Element Analysis, Computer Aided Engineering, Smart Products and HVAC.

Graduate of Naval Gunnery School as a Rocket Launcher Technician, 1979.

MILITARY EXPERIENCE

Gunners Mate Technician - U.S. Navy - 3/80 to 3/83 - Honorable Discharge.
* Duties included operating and maintaining a rocket launcher and gun mount. Handling Supervisor for nuclear and conventional weapons.

REFERENCES

An interview, references, transcripts and a detailed work history are available upon your request at the above address and phone number.

TAMINA G. RAWLEY
84 S. Banker Street • Santa Clara, CA 95021 • 805/555-4878

OBJECTIVE

A position with a hardware/software engineering development group, utilizing my experience as an Engineering Assistant and Electronic Technician, where education is encouraged and supported.

SYSTEMS
- State-of-the-art micro-based stand alone and multi-user workstations.
- UNIX-based networked terminals.

HARDWARE
- Computer Engines
- Graphic Engines
- Mass Storage Units

- Graphic Terminals
- Memory Controllers
- Displays

SOFTWARE
- UNIX
- MSDOS

- Word Perfect
- Microsoft WORKS

LANGUAGES
- Shell Script
- BASIC

- Assembler
- Custom Micro-Code

EXPERIENCE

TEKTRONIX, Sacramento, CA   1980 - 1993

Engineering Assistant/Support
Evaluated, qualified and supported a wide range of Workstation systems, graphic terminals and Mass Storage systems by upgrading, performing failure analysis, repairing and documenting information. Tested systems for Environmental and Mechanical specifications. Facilitated the ordering of equipment and parts to meet strict development time-lines.

Senior Electronic Technician
Maintained and repaired Workstation Systems, Graphic Terminals, Digital Analysis Systems and Storage Displays. Implemented quality improvement projects that have trimmed process times in the manufacturing environment. Worked closely with junior technicians and assemblers; helping them with electrical and mechanical problems as needed. Achieved expertise in Surface Mount Technology.

EDUCATION

Santa Clara University, Santa Clara, CA
Enrolled part-time in the Engineering Transfer Program   1984 - 1990
GPA 3.70/4.00   1993 - present
B.S. Degree anticipated March 1994

Albuquerque Technical Vocational Institute, Albuquerque, NM
Associate Degree in Electronic Technology
GPA 3.80/4.00   1978 - 1980

BARTHOLOMEW C. DECONCINI
723 S.W. Sixth Avenue
Detroit, MI 48112
(313) 555-9822

CAREER INTERESTS

A position with advancement potential in an engineering environment.
Would like this position to offer a challenge as well as an opportunity for
growth.

EDUCATION

Bachelor of Science Degree in Mechanical Engineering, Michigan State
University - December 1987.

DESIGN COURSEWORK
Computer Aided Design (AutoCAD)
Energy Efficient Building Design
Heating, Ventilation and Air-Conditioning, building systems -
S.E.A. program
Power Plant Design - energy conversion systems
Senior project - design, build, and race an entry in the Society of
Automotive Engineers Mini-Baja Competition

ANALYSIS COURSEWORK
Applied Stress Analysis
Materials Science
Fluid Dynamics
Vibration Analysis

COMPUTER EXPERIENCE
Numerical methods
Languages (Basic/FORTRAN)

PROFESSIONAL WORK EXPERIENCE

Project Engineer - Midwest Irrigation Systems - Detroit, Michigan
January 1988 - present
Design and cost estimation of commercial and residential irrigation
systems.

REFERENCES

Letters of reference and a course grade summary are available upon
request, or from:
Career Planning and Placement Center
Administrative Services Building
Michigan State University, East Lansing, MI 48824
(313) 555-1112

JUNE ROETHE, P.E.
8276 N.E. 163rd Street
Portland, Oregon 97243
(503) 555-1589

GOAL

To obtain an engineering position with a dynamic and growing company where I can use my analytical and computer skills to solve advanced engineering challenges.

EDUCATION

Master of Science, Mechanical Engineering
Portland State University, Portland, Oregon
(Currently working toward this degree; 75% completed; 4.0 GPA)

Bachelor of Science, Mechanical Engineering
Portland State University, June 1985
• Achieved a 3.8 GPA in engineering coursework.
• Completed full year of computer science coursework beyond the engineering requirement.
• Completed extensive independent study in finite element analysis using the ANSYS analysis
   package.

Areas of academic interest:
• machine design
• finite element analysis
• engineering application of microprocessors
• automatic controls
• computers in engineering

PROFESSIONAL EXPERIENCE

Project Engineer, ACME Robots and Manipulators, Portland, Oregon
November 1989 to present
• Responsible for new product development.
• Team leader for design of multi-tool hydraulic grinding manipulator for sale to USSR.
• Selected CPU and I/O components and performed preliminary panel layout as part of design
   team for digital robot and manipulator controls.
• Design hydraulic robot end effectors to meet customer specifications.
• Responsible for implementing CAD system for engineering department.
• Work with shop personnel to ensure ease of product manufacture and product costs within the
   budget.

Design Engineer, NDES Corporation, Mechanized Forest Products Division, Tacoma,
Washington
June 1987 to October 1989
• Designed hydraulically actuated attachments used for log skidding.
• Sole engineer responsible for designing new attachments that mount on crawler tractors.
• Created three dimensional layout of design using a Computer Aided Design work station.
• Analyzed kinematics with classical and computer methods.
• Performed stress analysis with classical and finite element methods.
• Worked with manufacturing personnel to ensure low cost and ease of product manufacture.
• Verified attachment fit at dealerships where prototypes are mounted.
• Analyzed product performance by observing prototypes in the field.

ROETHE - 2

COMPUTER EXPERTISE

Languages	*Operating Systems*
• C	• MS-DOS
• Turbo Pascal	• VMS
• Assembly	
• FORTRAN	
• Machine	
• BASIC	

Software:
• CADKEY (Computer Aided Design program)
• EXCEL spreadsheet
• AutoCAD
• Unigraphics
• NASTRAN (Finite Element Analysis package with GFEM for pre- and post-processing)
• Lotus 1-2-3 spreadsheet

PROFESSIONAL LICENSES

Professional Engineer, State of Oregon, 1990
EIT (Engineer In Training) exam passed, State of Washington, 1987

ACTIVITIES

President, Rose City Engineering Association, 1992-93
Chair, 1985 ASME Regional Conference
President, PSU ASME 1984-85

REFERENCES

Will be provided upon request.

David Riley   234 Bench Street, Denver, CO 80203 / 303-555-9876

Objective

To find a challenging job in one or a combination of the following areas; 1) Test 2) Sales/Service Engineering Support 3) Research 4) Design

Education

Bachelor of Science, Mechanical Engineering, University of Denver, CO - 1983 - GPA 3.68.

Course listing and/or official transcript available upon request.

Experience

9/93-present   **Caterpillar Corp., Denver, CO**

Product Engineer. 1/88-present.
Designed and specified detail parts for systems incorporated in fork lift trucks. Variety of systems include: Electrical, Hydraulic, Brakes, Operator Compartment design and other miscellaneous components required. Included finalization of bill of material listing and drawing clarification.

Maintenance Engineer. 9/86-12/87.
Corrected design, manufacturing or design problems as well as additions of new vendor products of current production lift trucks.

Sales and Products Engineer. 9/83-9/86.
Coordinated and provided specifications and technical information to Sales Department for use in sales literature. Extensive use of IBM compatible personal computers for spreadsheets, basic programming and word processing.

1980-1982   **US Army Corps of Engineers, Denver, CO**
Hydroelectric Design Branch

Engineering Technician. Summers.
Calculated preliminary & final performance evaluations on hydraulic turbines for government-owned hydroelectric facilities under supervision of project engineer. Corresponded with different turbine manufacturers for technical data.

Pertinent Information

Willingness to relocate and travel up to 40% of time.
Salary and benefits to be discussed at time of interview.
References available upon request.

JOSEPH PETRI
103 Stoney Brook Drive
Milwaukee, Wisconsin 53023
(414) 555-0371

QUALIFICATIONS SUMMARY

Over seven years of civil engineering experience. Over nine years of project management experience coordinating the feasibility, design, and construction of diversified municipal and industrial projects. These projects have been accomplished on time and within budget.

PROFESSIONAL EXPERIENCE SUMMARY

1989 to present
Waste Management, Inc., Milwaukee, WI
Position: **Engineering Project Manager**

> Developed new business involving hazardous waste remedial services with targeted industries and operations throughout the Pacific Northwest.

1983 to 1989
Cabel Michel Corporation, Milwaukee, WI
Position: **Engineering Product Manager**

> Planned and implemented a sales/marketing program for Newfibre® spunbonded, nonwoven, geotextile fabrics for protection of impermeable synthetic membranes in ponds, reservoirs, and landfills. Generated over $3,000,000 in new business.

1978 to 1983
Harper-Wade Engineering, Inc., Chicago, IL
Position: **Project/Construction Manager**

> Served as Project/Construction Manager for the "fast track" design and construction of a $24 million advanced waste water treatment plant, resulting in a project time reduction of nine months and a project cost savings of over $3,000,000. Also managed the permitting, design, and construction activities associated with development of a "grass roots" oil refinery, hydroelectric power plant, saw chain manufacturing plant, and semiconductor plant.

EDUCATION

Masters of Science, Civil Engineering, University of Wisconsin, 1978
Bachelor of Science, Civil Engineering, University of Wisconsin, 1976

PROFESSIONAL ASSOCIATIONS

> American Society of Civil Engineers
> Registered Professional Engineer

References Available Upon Request

Derrick W. Jefferson

27 West Panama, San Diego, CA 92132 / 619-555-4112

Objective   Refinery Engineer for major West Coast oil corporation

Professional Experience

1982 to 1993   **Caribbean Oil Refining Company,** Jamaica
Refinery Engineer

Coordinator and inspector of various capital improvement and maintenance projects for offshore oil tanker jetties and refinery buildings.

1977 to 1982   **Mobil Oil Company,** San Diego, CA
Corporation Engineering Department
Project Engineer

Project engineer for developing feasibility studies, appropriation cost estimates, and designs for 15 to 20 diversified onshore and offshore projects.

1973 to 1977   **Mobil Oil Company,** San Diego, CA
Oil Reclamation Division
Refinery Technician

Provided maintenance and troubleshooting for oil refineries in seventeen states. Worked with engineers on design issues. Helped identify and repair major component malfunction on refinery equipment.

Education

1972   **B.S. Chemical Engineering**
Pennsylvania State University, Hazleton, PA

Professional Associations

American Institute of Mining, Metallurgical, and Petroleum
Engineering
Association of Energy Engineers
American Chemical Society

References and detailed project history available upon request.

SHAWNA B. DAVIS
Tel: (206) 555-1930
30266 Fraser Creek Drive
Vancouver, WA 98623

SUMMARY

Extensive experience with progressively greater responsibility in varied managerial, project engineering and technical sales positions, with primary strengths in the areas of environmental technology, process equipment, industrial process control, engineering management and written and verbal communications. Also, in-depth design and project experience in the waste management field including the design and operation of energy recovery and recycling processes, and in the chemical, mining, and iron and steel industries.

OBJECTIVE

Project Manager / Project Engineer for industrial/municipal facility with focus on design, construction and operation. Willing to relocate.

EXPERIENCE

1991 to present
President/General Manager
Waste Products Corporation, Vancouver, WA

Responsible for the commercial development and facility design for a newly developed technology that converts municipal solid waste into an inert lightweight aggregate. Also took on a variety of consulting projects.

1989 to 1991
Chief Instrumentation Engineer/Project Engineer
Central Engineering Department, NACCO, Bellingham, WA

Duties: Responsible for coordinating the design, scheduling, procurement and estimating activities for the preparation of feasibility studies for new mineral processing facilities in Australia and Indonesia. This included supervision of outside consultants and numerous field trips to gather site and other relevant data.

1984 to 1989
Sales Supervisor, Project Engineer
Jenner & North, Inc., Seattle, WA

Duties: Responsible for the sale and execution of a number of major projects in the industrial automation field, primarily in the mining, iron ore pelletizing, steel and power industries.

1978 to 1984
Development Engineer
Taysom Engineering, Boise, ID

Duties: Responsible for the coordination required between the owners, consultants, government planning agencies, contractors and tenants on a number of commercial and industrial development projects.

DAVIS, p. 2

EDUCATION

1988
Master of Science Degree, University of Washington, Seattle
Civil Engineering, Part-time Executive Program

1978
Bachelor of Science Degree, University of Washington, Seattle
Electrical Engineering, Honors

ADDITIONAL DATA

Professional Engineer - States of Washington, Idaho
Computer literate in WordPerfect and Lotus 1-2-3
Excellent oral and written communications
Proposal and business plan preparation

DONALD S. SIMPSON
P.O. Box B235
Louisville, KY 40231
502/555-9219

EXPERIENCE

General Manager
Waste Management, Inc., Louisville, KY
1990 to present

Supervised all engineering and non-engineering staff members (48) at three solid waste treatment sites. Developed management plan for implementing coal-fired waste-to-energy facility. Served as chief engineer on design phase of project. Currently supervising construction phase.

President/Director
Environmental Resources Corporation, Memphis, TN
1988 to 1990

Responsible for the management of the business and its financing structure. Initially developed and implemented innovative technology for handling and processing municipal solid waste.

Engineering Manager/Vice President
Geometric Enterprises, Lexington, KY
1984 to 1987

Increasing responsibilities in the sales, design and execution of various projects under contract with the EPA, primarily in the chemical plant and waste management areas. Also responsible for the evaluation of a number of waste treatment facilities.

Industrial Process Control Consultant
Midwest Chemical Industries, Ltd., Frankfort, KY
1982 to 1984

Undertook process control systems design responsibility for a number of minerals processing plants being constructed by Midwest Chemical. This included the preparation of specifications, liaison with the clients, purchasing of equipment, supervision of installation and start-up.

EDUCATION

Bachelor of Science Degree, University of Alberta, Edmonton
1982, Chemical Engineering, First Class honors - two years

Bachelor of Science Degree, University of Kentucky
1988, Waste Management Technology

ADDITIONAL DATA

Professional Engineer - States of Kentucky and Tennessee
Available to travel and relocate

REVA GOLDSTEIN

2215 S. Median Way, Reno, Nevada 89503 • 702/555-4498

PROFESSIONAL OBJECTIVE

Seeking a Management position emphasizing acquired skills,
education and experience in the energy industry, including:

- General Management
- Operations Management
- Technical Management

QUALIFICATIONS AND ACHIEVEMENTS

Over 15 years of Engineering Management Experience
with primary emphasis and expertise in the following areas:

ENGINEERING OPERATIONS MANAGEMENT
- Large, Complex, Project Direction, Coordination and Definition
- Strategic Long/Short Range Planning
- Site Selection and Facilities/Plant Set-up
- Specific Expertise in Drilling, Mining Operations
- Research, Testing and Analysis

PERSONNEL MANAGEMENT
- Personnel Recruitment and Performance Evaluation
- Salary Negotiation and Administration
- Fostering Creative, Cooperative and Productive Employees
- Relationships in a Disciplined Work Environment

PROFESSIONAL EXPERIENCE

NEVADA DEPARTMENT OF ENVIRONMENTAL QUALITY - Reno, Nevada
Engineering Specialist (Jan. 1992 to Present)
Conduct Superfund hazardous waste site preliminary assessments
and site investigations. Monitor remediation activities and
response actions, review technical, design and other engineering
documents. Regulator for State and Federal Hazardous and
solid waste laws and regulations.

DENVER OIL PRODUCTION COMPANY
Denver, Colorado, 1985 to 1992
Technical Advisor to the Region Staff (1988 to 1992)
Monitored major drilling projects, coordinated corporate technical information;
involved with troubleshooting and quota evaluations.

Geologist, Group Supervisor (1985 to 1988)
Supervised 28 professionals and support staff. Formulated budgets, salary
administration, project definition and exploration strategy.

EDUCATION

UNIVERSITY OF NEVADA -- Las Vegas, Nevada
Bachelor of Science in Engineering Technology, 1983
Minors: Geology/Industrial Management

COLORADO SCHOOL OF MINES - Golden, Colorado
Department of Environmental Engineering
Completed intensive 29-week program on
Hazardous Waste Management, 1985

References Available Upon Request.

MOISHA V. DAHRENS
ENGINEERING CONSULTANT
Suite 13, 225 Austin Avenue S.W.
Houston, Texas 77012-7611
(713) 555-0277

OBJECTIVE

Seeking employment with growth-oriented engineering consulting firm, specializing in energy, chemical, and transportation industries.

SUMMARY OF PROJECT EXPERIENCE

◊ Developed procedures, checklists, and training protocols for implementing pre-loading inspections of rail tank cars and tank motor vehicles at DuPont manufacturing facilities.

◊ Led a geodetic engineering team to evaluate available toxic gas release computer models; acquired and improved a state-of-the-art modeling capability for DuPont and directed its application to DuPont facilities.

◊ Participated in environmental and safety compliance audits for numerous DuPont refineries, manufacturing facilities, wholesale terminals, and upstream production facilities in the U.S.

◊ Coordinated SEC environmental liabilities reporting for the Standard Oil Company, prior to the DuPont buy-out.

◊ Coordinated the establishment and propagation of the Chemical Education for Public Understanding Program (CEPUP) in-school systems in Texas via DuPont grant funding to the University of Texas at Austin.

◊ Coordinated DuPont's annual Engineering Expenditures Forecast, working with engineering departments in 27 manufacturing sites throughout the U.S.

EMPLOYMENT HISTORY

Senior Engineering Specialist, DuPont Southwest Region, Houston, Texas.
Jan. 1985 - present.

Engineering Specialist, Standard Oil Company, Energy Division, Austin, Texas.
Sept. 1980 - Dec. 1984.

EDUCATION

Bachelor of Science Degree, Chemical Engineering, University of Texas, San Antonio, 1980.

Certification, Geodetic Engineering, Professional Training Program, University of Texas, Houston, 1989. Also took extensive coursework toward certification in petroleum engineering.

References will be provided upon request.

Cal Fremont

127 Centerfield Drive, #23 • San Diego, California 92126 • (619) 555-2497

Professional Summary

More than 12 years of domestic and international experience in project management, engineering design, and construction supervision related to hydroelectric power, mining, and heavy civil projects.

Professional Experience

Marshfield Development Corp. - San Diego, California
Project Director - March 1985 to present

Managed multidisciplinary engineering effort and supervised constructibility reviews during preparation of design criteria, methodology, construction plans, and specifications for the Pacific Northwest National Gas Transmission System. Developed field surveillance and construction monitoring plans, reviewed Quality Control and Quality Assurance plans, and directly supervised construction of Northern Border and Pacific Transmission lines within system. Managed budget, subcontractors, schedules, and cost.

Senior Project Engineer - September 1980 to March 1985

Management and construction supervision of the Mission Hill hydroelectric project, which included: concrete and earth dams, control weirs and diversion tunnel; railway cuts, embankments, and bridges. Responsibility involved contract management, application of specifications, documents for tender, liaison with clients and public. Supervised rock and earth excavation, construction of coffer dams and grout curtain, installation of piezometer, pressure relief system, rock bolts, slope indicators, and other instrumentation. Supervised compaction and testing for earth dikes, concrete pouring and testing, and installation of dewatering systems. Also responsible for schedule, cost, and change orders. Assisted in design and construction supervision of many other projects, including:
- Rail and road tunnel beneath a navigational canal
- Four-lane highway tunnel, stretching 2 miles in granite
- Shipyard in southern Chile
- Highway bridges in Puerto Rico
- Hydro-electric power projects in Kenya, Argentina, and the West Indies

Education

B.S., Civil Engineering, University of California at San Diego, 1979.
Post-graduate certification training, Civil Engineering, UCSD, 1980.

References

Available, with detailed project descriptions, upon request.

Dana M. Keizer
2640 Maitland Circle SE
Hackensack, NJ 07603
(201) 555-3421

Objective

An advancement opportunity within a major engineering firm, with responsibility for project management and direction.

Skills & Experience

- Extensive background in engineering management and design of oil and gas pipelines, water resources, and hazardous waste management.

- Served as co-director for several major civil projects, including water, gas, and oil pipeline system design and construction.

- Experienced with managing business operations, profit centers, management information systems, and acquisitions.

- Managed responsibility for developing design standards and supervising implementation of quality control systems.

- Directly involved with site investigations and remediation designs for various project sites.

- Assisted with site characterization and feasibility studies and risk assessments.

Employment Summary

Northeast Development Corp. -- Newark, NJ -- 1989 - Present
Director of Technical Services, Engineering Division

DaVor Industries, Inc. -- Allentown, PA -- 1983 - 1989
Engineer, Special Projects Section

DaVor Industries, Inc. -- Wilmington, DE -- 1982 - 1983
Civil Engineering Intern

Education

University of Pittsburgh -- Philadelphia, PA -- 1983
B.S. Degree, Civil Engineering

Memberships

Registered Professional Engineer, NJ, PA, DE
Member, Geotechnical Society of America
Association of Civil and Mechanical Engineers

References   Available on request

TALBOT HUNTER
Rte. 6E, Stop 1156 // Chugiak, Alaska 99623 // (907) 555-3911

PROFESSIONAL OBJECTIVE

An Engineering Management position with a firm specializing in civil projects.

PROFESSIONAL EXPERIENCE

<u>Director of Technical Services</u>
Al-Can Engineering, Ltd., Anchorage, Alaska, 1987 to present

Supervised technical operations for regional offices in Alaska, British Columbia, and Alberta. Responsible for developing design standards, implementing project management and project control systems, and supervising construction at project sites. Worked with senior technical experts from all divisions, including chief engineer, chief hydrogeologist, chief compliance officer, chief construction manager, and the directors of bioremediation technology and health and safety.

<u>Executive Engineer</u>
Mentor GeoSystems, Inc., Anchorage, Alaska, 1984 to 1987

Prepared environmental impact statement, terrain sensitivity report, and design of river-crossing constructs. Prepared design manual for drainage and erosion control for Yukon Lateral Pipeline. Prepared final geotechnical report for submission to the federal government on the design and construction of the Trans-Canada natural gas pipeline.

<u>Engineering Specialist</u>
CH2M Hill, Engineering Consultants, Denver, Colorado, 1980 to 1984

Reviewed geologic, hydrologic, geotechnical, and thermal design for Trans-Canada natural gas pipeline. Assisted in establishing criteria for environmental protection, erosion control procedures, foundations, slope stability, surface and groundwater hydrology, design of drainage structures, and general civil construction techniques. Conducted detailed review of quality control plans. Provided on-site monitoring and technical assistance. Began employment as intern and was hired full-time upon degree completion.

EDUCATION

B. S. Civil Engineering, cum laude, University of Colorado, Denver, 1980

Founding member of student chapter of the American Society of Civil Engineers; served two years as president. Initiated program for on-site training and student internships with several local engineering firms, in cooperation with the College of Engineering.

REFERENCES AVAILABLE UPON REQUEST

Tina Chovanek

Current Address:
Souther Hall, Room 469
University of South Carolina
Columbia, SC 29208

Permanent Address:
1735 N. Paloma Blvd.
Charleston, SC 29401
Message phone: (803) 555-2481

Objective

To obtain an entry-level position with a firm requiring skilled technicians in the area of electronics engineering.

Education

Bachelor of Science Degree in Electronics Engineering
University of South Carolina, Columbia campus
Degree anticipated June 1994.
Current grade point average 3.75 overall/4.0 in degree courses.

Major areas of study:

- Electronic Systems
- Applications of Solid State Devices
- Engineering Analysis
- Integrated Circuitry
- Computer Programming
- Logic Design of Sequential Circuits

- Semiconductor Circuit Analysis
- Wave Shaping and Pulse Circuits
- Linear Network
- Digital Electronics
- Active Networks
- Electromechanical Laboratory

Work History

Lab Technician, Digital Electronics Laboratory, USC, 1992 to present

- Work closely with professors to develop sequence of experimentation and control studies for lower-division students.
- Assist with faculty research endeavors.
- Monitor equipment and supplies in facility and report shortages to office personnel.
- Supervise workers for safety practices.

Office Assistant, College of Electrical and Electronics Engineering, USC, 1990 to 1992

- Typed and proofread technical papers written by faculty for public presentation or publication.
- Supervised department office in absence of office manager.
- Managed telephone communications on 38-line system.

References

Provided on request, or available from USC Placement Office, Columbia, SC 29208.

**RESUME OF
THOMAS J. ZAMIR**

7715 Weston Park Lane
Charlotte, North Carolina 28214
704/555-2866

REGISTRATION

Registered Professional Engineer
American Institute of Chemical Engineers

EXPERIENCE

Seven years of experience in the engineering field, including managerial and program administration in land development, solid waste, and energy related projects. Types of projects included fossil fuel and hydroelectric generation, municipal waste landfills, and solid waste management planning. Technical experience includes development and preparation of engineering feasibility studies, regulatory licensing documents, siting studies, environmental impact assessments and environmental permitting. Managerial experience includes developing and implementing project manager techniques and tools, establishing project formats and protocols, developing and maintaining client contact, and reporting project progress.

RECENT ACCOMPLISHMENTS

Project Manager for the successful completion of a comprehensive and integrated solid waste management project for a central North Carolina county project. Included development of a Comprehensive Solid Waste Management plan; an Environmental Impact Statement; a Landfill Siting Study; and the preparation of detailed hydrogeologic investigation and engineering design that fulfilled the Solid Waste Management and Environmental Quality Review requirements of the State of North Carolina.

Assisted in the development and production of a Project Managers Manual for Moore EnviroTech, Inc. Responsible for compilation and review of the technical sections of the document as well as development and preparation of sample work plans and completed forms.

Speaker at two national conferences for two national associations—engineering and environmental—presenting the results of successful siting and permitting projects for solid waste facilities.

TECHNICAL AREAS OF EXPERTISE

Feasibility Study
Have performed both environmental and engineering feasibility studies for potential projects ranging from small sand and gravel mines to large hydroelectric and waste-to-energy facilities. Studies performed for private companies as well as government agencies, and in a number of states.

Siting Studies
Have conducted siting studies for potential facilities ranging from small solid waste management facilities to large hydroelectric facilities. Studies conducted for private companies, authorities, and governmental agencies.

Environmental Impact Assessment
Have conducted numerous environmental assessments and evaluations on projects as small as a 20 TPD solid waste transfer station to a large 1,200 Midwest nuclear generating facility. Have prepared numerous environmental impact statements In several states for both private companies as well as government agencies.

Communication Skills
Good communicative skills, including report writing, proposal preparation, and verbal articulation. Perform technical and editorial review for document consistency and presentation.

Managerial
Good technical supervisory skills, including planning, organizing, directing, and controlling projects. These are best exhibited on large-scale, long-term, multi-disciplinary projects.

EMPLOYMENT HISTORY

1986 - 1993 Moore EnviroTech, Inc., Charlotte, NC
Since 1990, Senior Environmental Engineer

1980 - 1986 Fisher & Parkfield Engineering Corporation, Syracuse, NY
Titled Engineer - Hydrologist

Education

M.S. - Chemical Engineering - Syracuse University (1986)
B.S. - Geological Engineering - Barton College (1980)

Sandra G. Patterson   //   77 W. 13th St.   //   Salt Lake City, UT 84121   //   (801) 555-2241

Career Objective	Entry-level engineering technology position in the field of industrial processes. Opportunity to train toward project management.
Education	Associate of Science Degree, Engineering Technology, 1992 New Mexico State University, Las Cruces, NM Currently working toward Bachelor of Science Degree in Industrial Engineering at the University of Utah; 70 percent complete.

Fields of Study

// Industrial Processes	// Fluid Technology
// Circuit Theory	// Control Systems
// Concrete and Soil Technology	// Applied Mechanics
// Thermal Power	// Applied Design
// Electronic Circuits	// Applied Strength of Materials
// Production and Quality Control	// Plant Design
// Systems Analysis	// Industrial Applications

Special Projects	Participated in team research program at local industrial processing plant. Served as team leader for plant analysis phase of project. Worked closely with industrial engineers and specialists in systems engineering. Assisted faculty member in development of lab technology program in electronic circuits lab. Prepared final paper that was submitted to state office of accreditation for approval.
Employment	Sales Associate, Radio Shack, Salt Lake City, UT 1990 to present Handle questions regarding product information and operation. Make sales of electronic equipment including computers, telephones, facsimile machines, and cables and components for do-it-yourself electronics projects.
References	Will be provided upon request. Transcript of college course work and course descriptions also available.

Paul E. Everett

Current Address: 7A West Hall, Providence College, Providence, RI 62028 • (401) 555-1242
Permanent Address: 8224 S. Marine Parade, Baltimore, MD 21217 • (301) 555-0112

Objective

Seeking a position in agricultural engineering with an organization working in irrigation and resources machinery.

Educational Background

Bachelor of Science Degree, anticipated June 1994
Providence College, Providence, RI
Major: Agricultural Engineering
Minor: Irrigation Engineering

Courses of Study

Irrigation System Design: Soil physics and plant water use applied to irrigation system design. Design of gravity, pressurized, and trickle systems; improving on-farm water management; performance characteristics of pumps and other irrigation equipment.

Soil and Water Conservation Engineering: Design of on-farm water supply and distribution systems, including wells, pipelines, and open channel flow. Hydraulics of soil profiles; design of drainage systems. Salinity management in agricultural production systems.

Biological Systems Modeling: Development of functional relationships using interpolation, regression, and cubic splines; development of models; stimulation of random processes; optimization techniques.

Design in Agricultural Engineering: The practice of engineering design, logical steps in the design process, emphasis on team approach to design, problem definition, iterative design.

Agricultural Structures and Environment: Load distribution, construction, and duration analysis; wood and reinforced concrete design; heat and moisture balancers; fasteners; mechanical and natural ventilation design; regular and controlled atmospheric storage.

Computers in Problem Solving: Engineering, physics, and chemistry problems solved through the use of sophisticated engineering software.

Other courses included: Design of Biological Resources Machinery, Groundwater Modeling, Applied Hydrology, Sediment Transport, Water Resources Analysis.

Employment History

Lab Assistant, Hydrology Laboratory, September 1992 to present
Providence College, Providence, RI

References available on request

D'LYNN KONDO * P.O. BOX 1983B * WILLISTON, ND 58801 * (701) 555-2496

CAREER OBJECTIVE

To obtain an entry level position as an engineering scientist with a large midwest corporation.

EDUCATIONAL EXPERIENCE

BS in Engineering Science, Ottawa University, Ottawa, Kansas, 1993
(GPA 3.75)

*   ELECTRICAL FUNDAMENTALS
    Electric theory laws. Circuit analysis of dc circuits. Natural, step, and sinusoidal responses of circuits. Operational amplifier characteristics and applications. Laboratory experimentation and analysis.

*   STATICS
    Analysis of forces induced in structures and machines by various types of loading. Involved in experimental processes under supervision of and in cooperation with graduate researcher.

*   DYNAMICS
    Kinematics, Newton's laws of motion, and work-energy and impulse-momentum relationships applied to engineering systems.

*   STRENGTH OF MATERIALS
    Properties of structural materials. Analysis of stress and deformation in axially loaded members, circular shafts, and beams, and in statically indeterminate systems containing these components.

*   THERMODYNAMICS
    Closed and open control systems. Thermodynamic theory, laws, properties; thermodynamic cycles, phase and chemical equilibria, and gas dynamics.

*   MATERIALS SCIENCE
    Structure and properties of metals, ceramics, and organic materials. Control of structure during processing and structural modification by service environment. Mechanical behavior of materials, relating laboratory results to material structure and elements of mechanical analysis.

*   MOMENTUM, ENERGY, AND MASS TRANSFER
    Control volume and differential analysis of fluid flow; momentum transfer; conductive, convective and radiative energy transfer; binary mass transfer; and prediction of transport qualities.

REFERENCES and official transcripts available on request.

JANE S. MILES • P. O. Box 128 • Linden, Alabama 36748 • 205/555-2095

OBJECTIVE

To obtain an entry-level position in chemical engineering within the paper or synthetic fibers industry.

EDUCATION

Bachelor of Science Degree, Chemical Engineering, 1993.
Purdue University, West Lafayette, Indiana.

Areas of Experience:

Convective Heat Transfer: Effects of convective heat transfer in gas solid systems; application to design of heat transfer equipment. Experimental laboratory experience.

Chemical Reactors: Design, performance, and scale of reactors involving solids (packed, fluidized, trickle, and slurry reactors) and without solids (gas/liquid absorbers, biochemical systems, non-ideal flow, polymerization systems).

Chemical Engineering Thermodynamics: Application of fundamental laws of thermodynamics to complex systems. Properties of solutions of non-electrolytes. Phase and chemical equilibrium. Chemical reaction equilibrium analysis and modeling for aqueous electrolyte solutions. Methods of estimating properties. Availability analysis.

Process Control: Analog and digital control methods and control strategies in the chemical process industries.

Special Projects:

Design and development of prototype heater/cooler method for stabilizing materials in production of high-opacity paper. Co-authored report to be printed in *Chemical Engineering Abstracts* in July 1994.

Honors project on the application of convective heat transfer properties to design of equipment to measure levels of condensation in paper production processes.

EXPERIENCE

Print Shop Technician, Magnolia Printing & Copy Center
Mobile, Alabama, 1988 to 1990

Worked as press operator on four-color sheet-fed printing press. Assisted with paper selection and purchasing. Familiar with basic properties of commercial-grade papers for printing.

REFERENCES
Will be provided upon request. Transcripts of college course work also available.

GINA A. PASTEGA
2125 N.W. Peoria Road
Burlington, Iowa 52602
(319) 555-3976

OBJECTIVE

Seeking employment in the field of chemical engineering where I can put my education to practical use for the benefit of a Midwest chemical corporation.

EDUCATION

Bachelor of Science Degree, conferred December 1993
Chemical Engineering with minor in pharmaceutical science
Ball State University, Muncie, Indiana
Cumulative Grade Point Average 3.56; Major/Minor GPA 3.87.

KNOWLEDGE AND SKILLS

Chemical Engineering Analysis
Experienced in laboratory and computer-aided analysis of chemical models for heat transfer, mass transfer, fluid flow, corrosion and corrosion control. Also prepared critical evaluation of models and solutions for problems in process flow sheeting, transport phenomena, reaction engineering, separations and process dynamics. Prepared extensive review of literature on current experimental work.

Chemical Plant Design and Chemical Reaction Engineering
Developed small-scale model of design for chemical plant; worked on design of chemical engineering equipment and developed working prototypes. Studied the design of chemical reactors, making comparisons of performance and economic evaluations of reactor types, with emphasis on single phase reacting systems.

Process Design and Control
Examined modern control theory and applied it to chemical systems. Experienced with identification, analysis, and control of processes using state-space and input-output methods in continuous and discrete time. Determined optimal design and operation of chemical processing systems, including large-scale and large number of variable type problems, mathematical methods, process modeling, constrained optimization and planning and scheduling problems.

Pharmaceutical Science
Experienced in applying quantitative methods, both chemical and physical, to pharmaceuticals and their dosage forms. Gained understanding of influence of pharmaceutical formulations on bio-availability of drugs; principles of pharmacology, pharmacodynamics, toxicity and pharmacokinetics.

WORK HISTORY

Student Intern, January to March 1994
Rexall Drug Store Pharmacy, Burlington, Iowa
On-the-job training in application of pharmaceuticals.

References available on request.

DAVID ALLISON

227 Winston Avenue
New Bedford, Massachusetts 02711
(413) 555-2719

PRIMARY OBJECTIVE
Full-time internship in civil engineering department of private or government agency.

EDUCATION

Bachelor of Science Degree, anticipated August 1994
University of New Bedford, Massachusetts

CLASSROOM / LABORATORY / FIELD EXPERIENCE AREAS

- Structural Theory
- Transportation Engineering
- Fluid Mechanics
- Soils in Engineering
- Surveying Theory
- Engineering Economics
- Highway Engineering
- Contracts and Specifications
- Statics
- Strength of Materials
- Materials Science
- Momentum
- Electrical Fundamentals

- Design of Steel Structures
- Civil Engineering Materials
- Hydraulic Engineering
- Applied Soil Mechanics
- Environmental Engineering
- Reinforced Concrete
- Hydrology
- Foundations for Structures
- Dynamics
- Thermodynamics
- Mechanical Properties of Materials
- Energy & Mass Transfer
- Statistics/Vector Calculus

SPECIAL PROJECTS

As part of a cooperative program with the Highway Department of the State of Massachusetts, I worked with highway engineers as they planned and designed a re-routing of Highway 8 from New Westport to Fairhaven, bypassing central New Bedford. My involvement was primarily as an observer, attending design meetings, site inspections and public hearings. Assisted with classification and identification problems. Participated in meetings and design problem-solving discussions.

REFERENCES/TRANSCRIPTS AVAILABLE ON REQUEST

Parker Jameson
116 S.E. Decker Terrace
Omaha, Nebraska 68101
(402) 555-0221

Professional Goal

To obtain entry-level employment in civil engineering with an organization involved in environmental management or conservation issues.

Educational Experience & Training

B.S. in Civil Engineering with Minor in Environmental Engineering
University of Omaha, Nebraska
Degree to be conferred June 1994

Engineering Qualifications:
Complete college-level training in the following subject areas:

Civil and Construction Engineering
Fluid Mechanics
Hydraulic Engineering
Civil Engineering Materials
Engineering Planning
Modern Construction Methods
Civil Engineering Design
Applied Structural Analysis
Probabilistic Structural Engineering

Environmental Qualifications
Complete college-level training in the following subject areas:

Environmental Engineering Fundamentals
Applied Hydrology, Water Resources Design, Ocean Engineering
Technology and Environmental Systems
Ports and Harbors
Air Pollution Control
Environmental Assessment
Earth Structures
Fate, Transport and Control of Hazardous Substances
Designing with Geotextiles
Soil Improvement, Soil Dynamics, Engineering Property of Soils
Applied Soil Mechanics
Water Quality Dynamics
Chemistry of Environmental Systems
Microbial Processes in Environmental Systems

References and course descriptions/transcripts available upon request.

DARRYL A MacKENZIE
442 NW Sunset Place
Corvallis, Oregon 97330
(503) 555-9227

CAREER OBJECTIVE

Civil engineering staff position in corporation or government organization responsible for large-scale civil construction projects.

DEGREE ACHIEVED

- B.S. Degree in Civil Engineering, 1993
- Oregon State University, Corvallis, Oregon
- Graduated 15th in class of 221; GPA 3.92
- Concentration: Major Project Design and Construction (Highways, Dams, Bridges)

SPECIALTY COURSES COMPLETED
(in addition to standard civil engineering requirements)

- Highway Engineering
- Highway Location and Design
- Reinforced Concrete Construction
- Low-Volume Road Design
- Asphalt Technology
- Advanced Concrete Technology
- Traffic Flow Analysis and Control
- Public Transportation Facility Design
- Transportation Systems Analysis and Planning
- Pre-stressed Concrete
- Traffic Operations and Design
- Bridge Design
- Construction Engineering Management and Methods
- Pavement Evaluation and Management
- Municipal Planning and Urban Engineering

EXPERIENCE

Student Internship, Summer 1992
State of Oregon Highway Division

- Worked with highway engineers on traffic pattern study and analysis.
- Conducted research in current traffic management theory and technology.
- Prepared written report for presentation to chief highway engineer.
- Assisted with planning and preparation for public hearings on proposed change in traffic flow.

REFERENCES on request.

Stephen Fairfield
P. O. Box 55
Santa Barbara, CA 93102
(805) 555-0993

Professional Objective

Seeking a position as engineering specialist with the engineering division of a major petroleum corporation.

Educational Training

Bachelor of Science Degree, anticipated March 1994
Civil Engineering with extensive course work in Ocean Engineering
University of California at Santa Barbara

Courses Completed

Fluid Mechanics I, II
Hydraulic Engineering I, II, III
Hydrology I, II, III
Ocean Engineering I, II, III
Water Resources Design I, II
Structural Theory and Advanced Structural Theory
Ports and Harbors: Design and Construction Methods
Photo Interpretation (with special study in interpretation of LANDSAT imagery)
Photogrammetry
Applied Structural Analysis
Water Quality Dynamics
Contemporary Engineering Technology
Dynamics of Ocean Structures
Applied Ocean and Coastal Engineering
Ocean Engineering Wave Mechanics
Random Wave Mechanics
Ocean Instrumentation and Control Theory
Wave Forces on Structures
Coastal and Estuarine Hydrodynamics
Ocean and Coastal Engineering Measurements
Finite Amplitude Wave Mechanics
Marine Geotechnical Engineering

Special Study

Prepared report on safety issues and design and construction solutions for offshore oil drilling platforms. Published in *Ocean Engineering Journal*, vol. 15, no. 3, Jan. 1994, pp. 137-139.

References and complete course descriptions and grade transcript will be provided on request.

Halimeda Shilaos
2212 Seminole Street
Tampa, Florida 33612
813/555-4356 (days)
813/555-2592 (evenings)

Career Objective

Project management position with large-scale construction projects for major engineering firm.

Educational Background

Bachelor of Science Degree, awarded June 1993
Construction Engineering Management/Civil Engineering

Specific Areas of Training Completed

Civil Engineering: Core requirements in civil and construction engineering, mechanics, statics, strength of materials, civil engineering design fundamentals, engineering economics, physics, calculus, materials science.

Construction Engineering Management: Plane surveying, fundamentals of estimating, dynamics for construction, fluid mechanics and hydraulics, construction estimating, construction project management, civil engineering materials, soils in engineering, structural theory, structural problems management, highway and road location and design, construction management, electrical and mechanical facilities, contracts and specifications.

Management and Business Principles: Management science, fundamentals of accounting, quantitative business methods, business law, legal issues in construction seminar, economics, business finance, managing organizations, accounting for decision making, management and labor.

Experience

Student Intern, Barry Brothers Engineering and Construction, Inc., Tampa, Summer/Fall 1993
Worked full-time under the supervision of the chief engineer on a major office complex construction project. Assisted in all areas of project management, including budgeting, scheduling, personnel management, record keeping, communications, and on-site management.

Framer, Castleton Construction, Tampa, Summers 1990-1992
Worked full-time as a framer for a residential construction company. Participated in the construction of more than 36 homes, including a 5,500 square-foot three-story structure and an 1,800 square-foot dome.

References available on request.

PETRA A. GALASHEN
98-A Huntington Park Drive
Long Beach, California 90822
Tel: (213) 555-4493

CAREER GOAL

Entry level position in the research and development department of an electronics manufacturing firm. Opportunities for advancement an essential element.

EDUCATION

- B.S. in Electrical and Electronics Engineering
  University of California, Los Angeles, 1994

AREAS OF CONCENTRATION

- Electronic Materials and Devices: Fundamentals of semiconductors, mathematical models, PN junction operation and device characteristics.

- Electromechanical Energy Conversion: Non-linear magnetic circuits. Saturable reactors and transformers. Voltage generation and energy conversion for electromechanical devices. Characteristics of electromechanical machines.

- Semiconductors: Semiconductor devices. Theories of PN and Schottky junctions. MOSFET, MESFET, JFET, and bipolar transistors. Theory and practice of semiconductor processing techniques. Semiconductor physics relevant for advanced use of semiconductor materials and devices. Quantum mechanics and solid state physics. Two- and three-terminal semiconductor electronic devices.

- Digital Electronics: Switching in electronic devices and circuits. Design and analysis of circuits in digital systems. Interconnections and noise problems. Theory and design of digital integrated circuits, including CMOS and bipolar logic. Analysis and design of digital integrated circuits. Digital signal processing. Optimum filter design, declamation and interpolation methods, quantization error effects, and spectral estimation. Digital image processing, enhancement and restoration. Encoding and segmentation methods.

WORK EXPERIENCE

Lab Technician, Electronics Laboratory, UCLA College of Engineering, Sept. 1992 to June 1994
- Worked with lab manager to maintain equipment and supplies, supervise lab sessions for pre-engineering students, and conduct equipment testing and servicing.

Library Aide, UCLA Engineering Library, Oct. 1990 to Sept. 1992
- Worked in circulation department. Responded to queries from library patrons. Shelved books and periodicals. Worked 25 hours per week in addition to full course load. Full-time in summers.

REFERENCES and course transcripts provided upon request.

Carole Van Sant • 336 Pritchard Street SE • Wichita, Kansas 67204 • 316/555-0118

Professional Objective

Entry-level position with growth-oriented computer design and manufacturing corporation.

Educational Experience

Bachelor of Science Degree in Computer Engineering, 1994
University of Arizona, Tucson, Arizona

Course Topics Covered

Calculus, Vector Calculus and Differential Equations
Programming Methodology
Digital Logic Design
Electrical Fundamentals
Statics and Dynamics
Data Structures, FORTRAN, COBOL, UNIX and C
Electric and Magnetic Fields
Electronic Materials and Devices
Electronic Circuits and Digital Electronics
Signals and Systems
Computer Organization and System Design
Microprocessor Applications
Computer Architecture
VLSI Design Techniques
Computer Operating Systems and Data Acquisition
Semiconductor Processes, Design, Devices
Power Electronics
Power Systems
Analog Integrated Circuits
Advanced Microprocessors

Special Studies

Designed and built personal 486 computer at 66 MHz, utilizing available materials in electronics laboratory with only a minor cost investment.

Wrote program that tests speed of microprocessor circuitry in nanoseconds. Prepared written report and sample operations for completion of senior honors project.

Work History

Central Computer Stores, Inc., Tucson, Arizona
Sales Associate, 1992 to 1994

Serve clientele in high-volume computer sales outlet store. Demonstrate equipment and software products.

References

Provided on request. Transcripts also available.

RUBY J. SANDERS

P. O. BOX 58, WELLS, NV 89835 (702) 555-3357

OBJECTIVE

An internship with an organization involved with resource management or conservation.

EDUCATION

Currently working toward Bachelor of Science degree in Minerals Engineering at the Colorado School of Mines, Golden, CO. Anticipated completion date, June 1994.

Courses Include:
- Mining Technology
- Metallurgical Engineering
- Mining Engineering
- Hydrology
- Instrumentation
- Computational Fluid Dynamics
- Environmental Engineering
- Mining Waste Treatment
- Chemical Structures Engineering

EXPERIENCE

Minerals Management Volunteer
Rocky Mountain National Forest
Central District
Mountain City, CO
July - Sept. 1993

Responsibilities Include:
- Assist forester in inspecting mining activities.
- Monitor reclamation and aspen regeneration studies.
- Help with recreation projects and administration.
- Perform minor maintenance duties.
- Participate in groundwater studies.

Assistant Night Manager
Dale's In and Out Drive-In
Wells, NV
Sept. 1990 to present

Responsibilities Include:
- Customer service and sales.
- Accurate cash tallies and inventory reports.
- Sole management of swing shift for small 24-hour restaurant.
- Personnel management and scheduling.
- Knowledge of all aspects of small restaurant operation.

REFERENCES ON REQUEST

GEOFFREY W. LAWRENCE
443 S. 26th St., Apt. 21
Salina, KS 67401
913-555-8861

CAREER GOAL

Entry-level position in the computer engineering department of a major electronics manufacturer.

EDUCATION

BS in Computer Engineering, Kansas Wesleyan University, Dec. 1993
Engineering program at KWU is E.A.C./A.B.E.T. Accredited
Degree conferred with highest honors

AREAS OF ACADEMIC SPECIALIZATION

Dynamic System Simulation

Digital, analog, and hybrid computer simulation of dynamic systems described by ordinary differential and difference equations.

Computer Architecture

Design techniques for the synthesis of digital computers. Principles of computer structure and design as applied to major computer functions. Internal organization and application of microprocessors and microcomputers. Design process for microprocessor systems. VLSI design theory and practice. Design, layout, and simulation of a complete VLSI chip using CAD tools.

Electronic Materials

Physics and chemistry of electronic materials and methods of materials characterization. Technology, theory, and analysis of processing methods used in integrated circuit fabrication. Advanced treatment of two- and three-terminal semiconductor electronic devices, microwave, and optical devices.

Integrated Circuits

Analysis and design of analog and digital integrated circuits. Advanced methods in digital, stochastic, and analog signal processing systems and system designs.

MEMBERSHIPS

Student Chapter, Institute of Electrical and Electronics Engineers
Student Chapter, National Action Council for Minorities in Engineering

REFERENCES PROVIDED ON REQUEST

Jerrold H. Carter
3220 Harrison Road
Austin, Texas 78759
512-555-2436

EDUCATION

Greenville College
B.A. cum laude, Mathematics, 1982
Greenville, Illinois

Technical:

The Cambridge Institute for Computer Programming
Certificate, 1984
Boston, Massachusetts

PROFESSIONAL EXPERIENCE - COMPUTER RELATED

Consultant Contractor/System Developer at IBM
10/91 - Present
Austin, Texas

• Contract developer on site at IBM. Architect of system
  implementation of a Smalltalk/VPM application of a OS/2 PM based
  computer network configuration system developed and marketed by
  IBM. Worked on project team of twenty as lead implementation
  designer and developer. Work included creating an OS/2 EE/ES DM -
  SQL-based object store, and object management of LAN and host-
  based connectivities. Beta tested VPM 2.0. Attendee: Digitalk
  Development Conference 91

Bit Stream Technology
Principal/System Developer
05/90 - 10/91
Scottsdale, Arizona

• Formed company to utilize object-oriented technology in building
  model-based software application systems. The focus was on both
  consulting and application delivery, with the language vehicles
  being Smalltalk/VPM/VW and C++. Development included an object
  description and management class system that facilitated rapid
  application development, especially with graphically based
  simulations. Specific application development was engineering
  related.

CH2M Hill
Systems Analyst/Micro Software Development
Corporate Information Systems
01/84 - 04/90
Denver, Colorado

• Lead corporate developer for microcomputer software system and
application design and programming with the emphasis on creating an
application development platform of re-usable high-level DBMS and
interface components. The systems architecture was object oriented
in construction with event-driven processing. It included a
spreadsheet user interface and data serving communications, both
asynch and ethernet, between MS-DOS/386 and VAX/VMS systems.
Language: 'C'. Experimented with Smalltalk-80, Smalltalk/286,
Macintosh, OS/2 PM SDK, and Windows SDK.

PROFESSIONAL EXPERIENCE - OTHER FIELDS

Alaska-Northern Contractors
Principal
08/78 - 12/79
Ketchikan, Alaska

• Ski-resort housing sub-contractor.

Bittner Industries, Inc.
Sales Representative
08/74 - 04/77
Dallas, Texas

• Responsible for a 12-state territory in art, photo, and framing
industries.

Carver J. Wood, P.C.E.
225 W. Vine Lane
Atwood, Tennessee 38220
615/555-2294

Professional Experience - Computer Systems Engineering

Vashon-Wells
Systems and Application Programmer
Graphics Products Center
07/86 - 1/87
Westport, Connecticut

• Worked on a plan of a systems level architecture for graphics products. The first four months of employment involved planning the data structures and user interface for a re-design of one of the graphics products - the map-making software MAP-MASTER.

VRAM Systems Inc.
Systems Analyst/Software Engineer
12/83 - 04/86
Cambridge, Massachusetts

10/84 - 04/86
• Lead designer of DBM in CAD/DBM system: An integrated CAD/database system was created with the DBM residing in a custom windowing system. The primary market for the system is architectural design and drafting. Languages: C and 286 assembler

07/84 - 09/84
• Assisted in planning a new architectural CAD system. Participated in creating system definition/design requirements. Evaluated HP-UX 3.xx on Series 200 hardware as well as Sun Microsystem hardware/Berkeley Unix. Tested the IBM-PC AT and various C compilers.

01/84 - 06/84
• Ported relational DBM/application development system: I licensed to SKOK a DBMS I developed. The system was ported from an IBM PC to Hewlett-Packard Series 200 equipment (68000 based) using the Pascal Operating System (2.1, 3.0). The system was marketed for $8,000 per user license as ARBASE. Languages: HP-Pascal and 68000 assembler.

Zen Tech Microsystems
Principal/Developer
07/82 - 11/83
Acton, Massachusetts

• Formed company to design, implement, and distribute a state-of-the-art DBM/application development system for 16-bit microcomputers. The principal market for the system was the small business user. As of 1986 the system was being marketed by four companies in Massachusetts. A source license was sold to SKOK Systems for use in conjunction with their architectural CAD system.

Edge Data Corporation
Microsystems Department Manager
10/81 - 06/82
Cambridge, Massachusetts

• Worked as a consultant in the design of software and the designation of hardware requirements for high end microcomputer systems. Programming was done in Pascal and 8086 assembler.

HH Aerospace Design Co. Inc.
Consulting Programmer
02/81 - 09/81
Bedford/Cambridge, Massachusetts

• Worked on a team modifying the ARTS IIIA air traffic control system to include a conflict alert capability as specified by FAA contract. The programming was done in UNIVAC ULTRA assembly language on a real-time, multi-processing system of seven IOP processors.

Professional Experience - Other Fields

Center High School
Teacher
08/77 - 08/78
Hadley, Missouri

• Instructed all high school mathematics classes.

Adult Education Center
Instructor
01/71 - 08/73
East St. Louis, Illinois

• Developed a curriculum in mathematics for a complete, intensive high school level course, which was later adopted by a local junior college.

Education

B.S. Computer Engineering, Wentworth Institute, Boston, Massachusetts

Additional Information

• Maintaining a strong interest in the uses of microcomputer technology.
• Active in developing investment software applications for personal use.
• Prior member of the Boston Computer Society.
• Graduated first in a class of 180 in college; captain of the tennis team.
• Travel - Australia, New Zealand, Cook Islands, Tahiti.

Thomas K. Lewis
Route 3, Box 112-5
Big Timber, Montana 59011
(406) 555-4730

Career Opportunity Sought

Entry-level position in forest land management and operations,
with specific interest in watershed and soil stabilization management.

Educational Background

Bachelor of Science Degree, 1994
Forest Engineering
Humboldt State University, Arcata, California

Curriculum Included the Following:

Full complement of mathematics, biochemistry, and physics courses.
Advanced Forest Surveying
Forest Engineering Computations
Tree Identification
Wood Technology
Engineering: Statics, Strength of Materials
Forest Biology
Forest Mensuration
Harvesting Processes
Logging Mechanics and Management
Engineering Properties of Forest Soils
Forest Soil Mechanics
Operations Analysis
Watershed Processes
Forest Engineering: Fluid Mechanics and Hydrology
Reforestation
Physical Geology for Engineers
Logging Structures and Roads
Production Planning and Management
Harvest Area Planning and Implementation
Forest Resource Economics
Amenity Resource Management
Forest Policy
Principles of Silviculture

Employment Experience

Volunteer Surveyor, U.S. Forest Service, Humboldt National Forest
Part of Student Internship Program, HSU, Summers 1990 to 1993

Amelia Gomez-Nacio
- 227 N.W. "C" Street
- Phoenix, Arizona 85021
- 602-555-9930

Position Objective
- Aeronautical engineering position with major aeronautics laboratory.

Previous Employment
- Aerodynamics Engineering Technician
- Satellite Operations Center, Scottsdale, Arizona
- June 1988 to August 1992
- Responsibilities Included:

   Involvement in aero/thermal engineering, aerodynamics, thermodynamics, and fluid mechanics programs. Testing low-speed incompressible to hypersonic flows in both analytical and experimental developments. Prepared system concept studies, detailed analyses. Monitored laboratory and wind tunnel testing and flight testing. Specific projects included the development and testing of hypersonic reentry configurations, gas-dynamic laser flow facilities, aerodynamic control of high-power laser propagation, and the analysis and measurement of aerodynamic phenomena affecting the performance of ground-based and airborne sensors.

- Engineering Intern
- Los Alamos Laboratory and Testing Center
- Los Alamos, Nevada
- June to September 1987
- Responsibilities Included:

   Assisting aerodynamics, electronics, mechanical, and astronautical engineers in varying aspects of testing assessment and analysis. Role on team was primarily as observer. Participated in planning and design meetings. Maintained record-keeping files for three departmental engineers.

Education
- 1993: Master of Science, Aeronautics Engineering, University of Nevada, Las Vegas

- 1988: Bachelor of Science, Aeronautics Engineering, Embry-Riddle Aeronautical University, Daytona Beach, Florida

References on request

Stuart G. Davies • 22785 S.E. Bascomb Road • Rogue River, Oregon 97502 • 503/555-9112

- Professional Objective: Forest Engineering position with major timber corporation.

- Educational Background: Bachelor of Science Degree, Forest Engineering/Civil
  Engineering, University of the Southwest, Phoenix, Arizona
  Degree awarded December 1993; graduated 6th in class of 120.

- Areas of Academic Training:

  - Forest Transportation Systems: Analysis of interactions between harvesting and road
    systems. Road and landing spacing, determination of road standards, analysis of
    logging road networks, transfer and sort yard facility location. Simultaneous resource
    scheduling and transportation planning. Fixed and variable transportation cost
    economics as applied to transportation issues.

  - Logging Mechanics: Relationship of torque, power, and thrust to the operation of cable
    and ground harvesting systems. Fundamentals of cable logging system performance,
    properties of wire rope, load-tension relationships, payload calculation, and carriage
    design. Analysis of lateral yarding and slack pulling forces, guyline production and
    spar tree analysis, interlock design, estimating, production using physical models.

  - Forest Engineering Operations Management: Harvest unit optimization; optimization of
    equipment replacement, scheduling and selection. Applied analysis using linear
    programming, integer programming, dynamic programming, network techniques, non-
    linear program, iterative techniques, and simulation. Identification and measurement
    of production components in harvesting systems, heavy equipment operations, and
    crew type activities. Methods analysis, productivity improvement, and engineering
    economics. Strategic planning of transportation systems using network theory. Report
    writing and oral presentation.

  - Production Planning: Resource planning using critical path analysis, linear
    programming, and tactical approaches. Analysis of alternatives using benefit foregone,
    intangibles, and regulations. Business planning, including bidding, budgeting,
    scheduling, inventory control, equipment replacement analysis, and fleet
    maintenance.

  - Forest Surveying: Plane surveying using forestry problems. Low-order surveying with
    compass, abney, clinometer, and hand-level. U.S. Public Land Survey System,
    topography, and mapping. Directional instruments, electronic distance measurements,
    field astronomy, State Plane Coordinate Systems, horizontal control, specifications,
    triangulation, and trilateration. Survey law.

- Previous Work Experience: Timber worker, Johnson Brothers Logging Co., Rogue River,
  Oregon, 1981 to 1989. Experienced with all areas of logging operation, including
  felling, yarding, slack pulling, guyline, spar setting, and loading.

- References provided upon request. Course transcripts also available.

RESUME FOR:

PAT WAHANA
445 W. Fifth Street
Raleigh, North Carolina 27612
919/555-4820

OBJECTIVE: Industrial Engineering Management

EXPERIENCE: Industrial Engineer
E-Systems, Inc., ECI Division
Raleigh, North Carolina
1986 to present

Responsibilities Include:
Design and initiate all stages of production process.
Design and installation of assembly lines and procedures.
Automated production and testing.
Experienced with most advanced testing equipment currently
available.
Quality control operations; ensure products and systems meet required
specifications.
Analyze failures or defects to determine necessary corrective
measures.
Installation, maintenance, and modernization of plant facilities.

Industrial Engineer
Emerson Electric Co.
St. Louis, Missouri
1984 to 1986

Responsibilities Included:
All phases of production, budgeting, and scheduling.
All aspects of procurement and planning for manufacturing areas.
Testing and troubleshooting of manufacturing processes.
Training of new engineering hires.

EDUCATION: B.S. Industrial Engineering
Wake Technical Institute
Raleigh, North Carolina
Degree Awarded June 1984

MEMBERSHIPS: Society of Women Engineers, North Carolina Chapter
American Institute of Plant Engineers
American Institute of Industrial Engineers
North Carolina Association of Industrial Engineers
North Carolina Women in Business

REFERENCES: Provided upon request

Miguel Sifuentes
3290 S.W. Arches Street
Pueblo, CO 81030
(303) 555-2286

Job Objective

Mechanical Engineering Position with Major Manufacturing Corporation.

Related Work Experience

Mechanical Engineer
Allied Industrial Systems
Pueblo, CO
Jan. 1983-Nov. 1993

Responsible for all phases of mechanical design and development of sophisticated equipment used in transportation—from ships to space shuttles. High level of accuracy essential. Oversaw production design with industrial engineers. Worked with production chief to determine optimal methods for production. Assisted with departmental budget preparation and implementation.
Plant closed Nov. 1993.

Mechanical Engineer
AN/APG, Inc., Government and Defense Group
Denver, CO
June 1978 to Jan. 1983

Responsible for variety of duties on physical design projects, including airborne, ship borne, or land. Handled stress analysis, fracture analysis, and product improvement design of all the electromechanical servomechanisms. Designed hydraulic systems, performed testing, and prepared specifications and proposals. Worked closely with electrical and manufacturing engineers and technicians.

Technician, Mechanical Engineering Division
AN/APG, Inc., Industrial Group
Denver, CO
June 1977 to June 1978

Worked half-time while completing training for Professional Mechanical Engineer Certificate. Assisted mechanical and manufacturing engineers with analyses, testing, and mechanical drafting.

Education

B.S. Mechanical Engineering, June 1977
Pueblo University, Pueblo, CO

Certification Training/Testing, American Society of Mechanical Engineers
State of Colorado, Denver, CO

Jake Markham
443 W. Emerson Drive
Concord, New Hampshire 03301
603/555-8991

Employment Objective

Seeking a position as a senior electronics engineer with a company involved with the design of electronic systems.

Previous Work Experience

Electronics Engineer, *J&G Industrial Electronics, Inc.*
Concord, New Hampshire
June 1985 to present

Responsibilities include: Design hardware, interface, test, analyze, and evaluate microprocessors. Operate, design, and test microcomputer-based instrumentation systems. Research automatic test systems, radar systems, and guidance systems. Research performance statistics on complete systems. Work with both analog and digital systems.

Digital Electronics Engineer, *Digital Enterprises of New Hampshire*
Manchester, New Hampshire
June 1983 to June 1985

Responsibilities included: Design digital circuitry on microprocessor applications, high-speed multiprocessor computer architecture, digital signal processors, and bit mapped graphics. Concerned with real-time applications, micro-programming, assembly language, and high-level language. Special projects involved image processing, signal/data processing, control/servo systems, test systems, and artificial intelligence. Contributed to projects on fire control systems and electronic intelligence devices.

Education

Bachelor of Science Degree, Electronics Engineering
University of Manchester, New Hampshire
Degree Awarded June 1983

Served as president of student chapter of Institute of Electrical and Electronics Engineers for two years. Actively involved in Engineering Honor Society, organizing speakers and presentations by faculty on special topics. Coordinated placement assistance program for electrical and electronics engineering students in cooperation with career counseling department on the campus.

References provided on request.

Daniel Evans Creighton
1442 S. Jefferson Street
Brattleboro, Vermont 05351
802-555-6648

Objective

Position as ceramic engineer with manufacturing corporation.

Previous Employment

Ceramic Engineer, Champion Spark Plug Company, Toledo, Ohio
Employment Dates: August 1988 - January 1994

Involved in the development of new ceramic bodies, materials processing, and quality controls for the development and production of spark plug insulators. Conducted studies on glass, semiconductors, glazes, high-temperature sealants, and cements. Developed strategy for testing procedures that saved 15 percent in costs annually and increased testing accuracy and efficiency by 45 percent.

Materials Engineer, Avco Systems, Textron, Wilmington, Massachusetts
Employment Dates: September 1980 - July 1988

Developed advanced materials for heat protection systems applications. Synthesized plastic, ceramic, and graphite composite constructions, including high-temperature processing procedures. Responsible for analysis, reliability, maintainability, safety, planning, and conducting all formal system-level testing.

Educational Background

Bachelor of Science, Materials Engineering, University of Massachusetts, Amherst
Degree Date: August 1980

Graduate course work completed in ceramics engineering, University of Toledo
Enrollment Dates: September 1988 - June 1989
Completed 65 percent of work required for Master of Science degree

Memberships

American Ceramic Society
American Society for Testing and Materials
Ohio Council for Industrial Engineers (former)
Engineering Society of Massachusetts (former)

References on Request

Jane Bessington • 18 West Court Street • Shreveport, Louisiana 71102 • 318-555-6510

Objective

Electronics engineering position with innovative communications corporation.

Education

Bachelor's degree in Electronics Engineering
University of Louisiana, Baton Rouge
Degree Awarded 1992

Engineer-In-Training (Certification)
ACI and Associates, New Orleans, Louisiana
Certification/License Pending

Occupational Experience

Electronics Engineer Technician (Engineer-In-Training)
ACI and Associates, New Orleans, Louisiana
Dates of Employment: June 1992 to June 1993

Responsibilities included:
- Testing of electro-optical analog and digital processors.
- Review of design and technology for microprocessors.
- Analysis of signal processing identification and warning systems.
- Digital analysis study preparation.
- Assist with testing and predictions of mean-time-between-failure rates (MTBF).
- Assist electronics engineers in preparation of components.
- Attend training sessions in electronics engineering for the professional.

Memberships

Institute for Electrical and Electronics Engineers, Student Chapter, ULBR
ULBR Engineering Honor Society
Student Coalition for Responsible Science and Engineering

References

Available upon request. Official university transcripts also provided on request.

Abdul Gassazi Murza
224 West Fourth Street
Albany, New York 12211
518/555-6428

Position Desired:

Aeromechanics engineering position with manufacturer of commercial or military aircraft. Willing to relocate anywhere in the United States.

Education:

M.S. Aerodynamics and Engineering Design, 1993
Wentworth Institute, Boston, Massachusetts

B.S. Aeromechanics Engineering, 1991
Kansas Technical Institute, Salina, Kansas

Areas Studied:

Dynamics: Aeroelastic loads and stability. Dynamic test and evaluation.

Aerodynamics: Aerodynamic and performance analysis. Preliminary design analysis. Wind tunnel test program design. Development of aerodynamics analysis tools.

Stability and Control: Qualities analysis and design. Flight simulation testing design and analysis. Development of real-time simulation models. Integration of feedback advanced flight control laws.

Structural Dynamics: Test vibrations, dynamics loads. Aeroelastic stability of materials. Layout and design of mechanical structure materials, parts, and components.

Experience:

Research Associate: Under Dr. Malcolm Fisher, Research & Development Department, Wentworth Institute, Boston, Massachusetts, 1991-1993

Conducted research and experimentation on aeroelastic properties of various materials. Prepared detailed reports on test results. Analyzed data sets with linear and non-linear methodology. Assisted with writing of final report for publication.

References:

References, publications, and transcripts will be provided upon request.

K.J. Butters
2276 La Center Blvd.
Gainesville, FL 32601

OBJECTIVE

Quality control management position in the energy industry, preferably hydro-electric power or solar power development.

EXPERIENCE

Quality Control Supervisor
Florida Power & Electric
Nuclear Division
Gainesville, FL
June 1986 to present
- Program planning and data evaluation; quality control supervision in all areas of operation, design, and production in compliance with the requirements of the Nuclear Regulatory Commission and other regulatory agencies.
- Assist in licensing review activities and coordinate all licensing aspects of projects.
- Thermal analysis, thermal/fluid dynamics analysis of water, gas, and liquid-cooled reactor cores.
- Random testing and evaluation of instrumentation control.
- Evaluation and testing of operations procedures and safety procedures.
- Random screening of emergency management procedures.
- Supervise staff of 7 engineers and 5 engineering technicians.
- Cooperate with nuclear engineers in testing and maintenance programs.
- Provide quality assurance training to all new operators.
- Coordinate safety and quality control communications for 7 reactor facilities.

Nuclear Engineer
Florida Power & Electric
Nuclear Division
Orlando, FL
June 1982 to June 1986
- Thermal analysis and thermal/fluid dynamics design and testing.
- Stress and structural analysis of reactor components.
- Design and testing of reactor core components.
- Systems design and analysis.
- Manage activities of the maintenance department and provide technical supervision to ensure the safe, reliable, and efficient operation of the nuclear plant.
- Review, investigate, analyze, and interpret data on costs, manpower, materials, and schedules in support of project management.

EDUCATION

BS, Nuclear Engineering, 1982
Pennsylvania State University, Altoona

REFERENCES

Provided on request

James P. Archer
12267 W. Starker Drive
LaCenter, Washington 98629
(206) 555-0029

Position Objective

Mechanical engineering position with construction or manufacturing.

Professional Experience

Mechanical Engineer
Washington Pacific Power Supply Corporation
Seattle, Washington
1983 to present

Coordinate additions to and alterations and retirements of
corporate facilities. Serve as consultant on design,
construction, and operating problems. Make engineering studies
and assist with research and development plans to achieve the
most economical expansion of the corporation's physical plant
operations in the mechanical engineering fields. Inspect and
conduct tests on mechanical equipment to determine if it meets
the required specifications. Responsible for quality control of
construction operation at two new plant sites.

Mechanical Engineering Specialist
Bonneville Power Station
Bonneville, Oregon
1980 to 1983

Coordinate power plant loading. Analyze plant efficiency and
cost data to effect optimum use of facilities in power
production. Operate, maintain, and measure performance of on-
line power stations along Columbia River. Work as
instrumentation and control engineer as needed for relief.

Education

BS Mechanical Engineering
University of Washington
Seattle, Washington
Awarded June 1980

Special Training in Energy Engineering, Safety Control, Quality
Assurance, and Engineering Economics through American Institute of
Mechanical Engineers.

Memberships

American Institute of Mechanical Engineers
Association of Energy Engineers
Northwest Energy Engineers Coalition

References on request

Gerald McCaig, P.E.
2259 Queen Street, S.E.
Allentown, PA 18101
814/555-2293

Career Goal

Senior Electrical Engineering position within the energy production industry.

Employment Experience

1988-present
Electrical Engineer
Pennsylvania Power & Light Company
Allentown, PA

Assist in preparation of plans for development and expansion of company facilities operations. Development, design, and implementation of computer procedures that apply engineering and mathematical techniques to solving complex technical problems. Planning, design, and construction supervision of three new electrical facilities. Reviewing plants for potential improvements. Preparing plans, designs, and maintenance schedules to implement improvements. Experienced with instrumentation control engineering for operation of boilers, turbines, and other power plant (non-nuclear) equipment. Perform and direct electrical tests required to place and maintain in service the automatic and manual control distribution systems in the eastern Pennsylvania territory. Plan, schedule, and conduct voltage surveys. Operate, maintain, and measure the performance of on-line power stations.

1987-1988
Engineer-In-Training
PP&L
Allentown, PA

Worked as special assistant to senior electrical engineer during work in training program toward licensing and certification. Assisted with all aspects of electrical engineering work in power generation and relay stations.

Education

1987
BS in Electrical Engineering
University of Pennsylvania, Allentown

Memberships

Institute of Electrical and Electronics Engineers
Society of Pennsylvania Electrical Engineer

References on request

JARRED W. CONLIFF

4644 Southwest Marine Drive
Stoneybrook, California 94311

(810) 555-3488
FAX (810) 555-3498

OBJECTIVE

Seeking a position in waste control engineering with responsibility for facilities management.

QUALIFICATIONS SUMMARY

Petrophysical engineer with strengths in treatment and disposal of hazardous and toxic waste, analyzing natural and occupational environments for pollution, managing waste remediation, planning disposal and treatment of hazardous waste, designing and operating air and water pollution control equipment, and administering waste management systems.

PROFESSIONAL EXPERIENCE

California-Pacific Power Company   1987 to present
La Jolla, California
General Field Engineer

- Managed hazardous waste remediation program for nuclear waste water from four facilities.
- Designed water pollution control units for relay stations.
- Earned three promotions in four years through corporate training and development programs.
- Established computerized tracking system for waste removal program.
- Monitored air and water pollution levels for three-county territory.
- Developed and implemented plans for corrective measures on air and water emissions.
- Voluntarily instituted tougher standards for emissions.
- Trained field engineers in pollution evaluation and control.

American Marine Drilling Corporation   1982 to 1987
San Diego, California
Engineering Technician

- Responsible for designing and directing drilling operations from start up to dismantling.
- Trained in hazardous waste shipping and chemical containment.
- Monitored marine geophysical research reports and incorporated relevant information into design and operations plans.

EDUCATION

BS, Petrophysical Engineering   1981
Colorado Institute of Mineral Science and Technology
Mountain Park, Colorado

REFERENCES ON REQUEST

Patrick J. Allan

17 East Moreland Drive
Chicago, Illinois 60611

Tel: (312) 555-2298
Fax: (312) 555-2192

Registration:

- Licensed Professional Engineer, State of Illinois

- Certified Environmental Professional, National

Recent Accomplishments:

- Served as project manager for the successful completion of a comprehensive integrated solid waste management project for Will County, south of Chicago.

- Assisted in the preparation and implementation of a land use development plan for the State of Illinois, in cooperation with the Land Development Commission, the Environmental Protection League, and the Federal Bureau of Land Management.

- Prepared and directed engineering feasibility study, including environmental impact statement, for siting of water treatment facility.

Employment History:

1985 - 1992   Templeton Engineering Consultants, Inc.
                 452 East Stewart Avenue, Suite 112
                 Chicago, Illinois 60612
                 Senior Engineering Consultant

1981 - 1985   M.W.N. Engineering Associates, Ltd.
                 Parker Building, Suite 2600
                 24th and Madison
                 Chicago, Illinois 60602
                 Engineer - Hydrologist

1977 - 1981   Tensor Industries, Inc.
                 144 West Marquam
                 Chicago, Illinois 60626
                 Engineering Technician

Education:

1977   L.P.E. Course, Central Technical Institute
1976   B.S., Geological Engineering, Wheaton College

References: Upon request

Jonathan Hooper • 7728 S. Coruna Street • Santa Fe, NM 87502 • 505-555-2497

Current Objective

Project management position with an engineering technologies consulting firm.

Summary of Qualifications

Expertise in the areas of waste-to-energy and waste recovery technology solutions, recycling technology, testing and analysis of groundwater levels and flow, and electric power generation technologies. Excellent written and oral communications skills and thorough knowledge of current environmental regulations for federal and state policy makers.

Recent Project Experience

Project Manager for Santa Fe Environmental Systems Waste-to-Energy Feasibility Study - Preparation of an analysis of the solid waste management practices of the Santa Fe regional facility, coupled with an environmental assessment of a potential site to determine the feasibility of developing a waste-to-energy facility in Lamy, NM. Developed engineering design for facility currently under construction.

Consultant/Project Manager, Department of Sanitation, Santa Fe - Preparation of a feasibility study (environmental fatal flaws, geotechnical analysis, engineering constraints, hydrogeologic analysis) for the proposed redevelopment of the closed San Felipe Landfill for use as an ash residue disposal site for the city's solid waste incinerators and proposed waste-to-energy facilities.

Project Engineer, Southeast Project - Development of engineering design and permit information for development of a major fossil-fuel fired electric generating facility.

Lead Environmental Analyst for the County Energy Management Committee - Designed study to perform environmental impact comparative analysis of current coal generators versus waste-to-energy incinerator-generators. Study published in national professional journal.

Work History

1988 - present: Consultant, Enso Engineering Associates, Santa Fe, NM
1986 - 1988: Hydrologist, New Mexico Department of Energy, Albuquerque, NM
1982 - 1986: Research Associate, University of New Mexico, Albuquerque, NM

Education

1982: Bachelor's degree in Hydrology Engineering, University of New Mexico, Albuquerque
1983: Professional Engineer License Examination Completed

References on request

Trent Howard
149 N.E. Goshen Drive
Fredericksburg, VA 22405
703/555-6265

EMPLOYMENT OBJECTIVE

Engineering consultant for water resources management organization.

EDUCATION

M.S. Water Resources Engineering
Virginia Technical Institute, 1991

B.S. Civil Engineering (Minor in Water Resource Engineering)
Purdue University, 1988

WORK HISTORY & EXPERIENCE

Research Associate, Virginia Technical Institute, 1988 to present

Hired as associate to Research and Consulting Division of VTI, working on a variety of special projects, including:

- Georgia Rivers Study: Navigability investigation of the streams and rivers within the civil works area; under contract to the U.S. Army Corps of Engineers in Savannah, Georgia.

- Alaska Rivers Study: Navigability investigation of the streams and rivers crossed by the Trans-Alaska Oil Pipeline; under contract to the U.S. Army Corps of Engineers, Alaska District.

- Wetlands Study: A comparative analysis of methods of identifying freshwater wetlands; under contract to the U.S. Army Corps of Engineers, Adirondack District.

- Upper Roanoke River Basin Study: Navigability, water flow, and water quality investigation of waters of the Upper Roanoke River Basin; under contract to the State of Virginia, Department of Water Resources.

- Headwater Pilot Program: Hydrologic analysis of small headwater streams to determine selection of cfs location along the Upper James River, Virginia; under contract to the State of Virginia, Department of Water Resources.

MEMBERSHIPS

Water Resources Institute of Virginia
American Water Resources Association

Complete references will be provided on request.

WALLACE D. MAMAKA
334 Terra Lane • Denver, Colorado 80212 • 303/555-6675

CURRENT EMPLOYMENT OBJECTIVE

Engineering specialist position with responsibility for
permitting procedures for mining corporation.

RELEVANT EXPERIENCE

Developed a program for the reclamation of boreholes
and excavations for feasibility of developing a coal mine.

Conducted site analysis and prepared list of permit
requirements for development of major oil shale project.

Prepared a historical summary of heavy oil mining
efforts and comparison of present-day methods.

Coordinated environmental impact analysis and drafted statement
for the development of a 25-acre sand and gravel mining operation.

Prepared a hard-rock mining reclamation plan with applicable
permit documents and supplemented with traffic and noise studies.

Instituted permit procedures for the relocation (excavation and filling)
of soil within a 100-year flood plain for designated recreational river corridor.

EMPLOYMENT HISTORY

Mining Engineer, Sandview Mining Corporation
Denver, Colorado, 1983 to present

Engineering Technician, Mobil Oil
Los Angeles, California, 1978 to 1980
Denver, Colorado, 1980 to 1983

EDUCATION

Colorado State University, Fort Collins
M.S. Mining and Metallurgy Technology, 1978
B.S. Geology, 1976

REFERENCES

Provided on request.

Chapter Six

SAMPLE COVER LETTERS

HUNTER BOTTJER • 2254 W. Brick Street, Apt. B4 • Anchorage, AK 99510 • 907/555-2247

Davison Jackson
Division Manager
Product Engineering
Alaskan Metals & Manufacturing
P.O. Box 23W
Fairbanks, AK 99704

Dear Mr. Jackson:

Thank you for the time you spent discussing the position as your associate at Alaskan Metals & Manufacturing. I am submitting this letter and the enclosed resume in formal application.

After our conversation, I felt strongly that this is a position that I can fill with energy and enthusiasm. I bring to it more than a dozen years of professional experience as a drafter, including five years in supervisory positions. I understand the critical issues of accuracy and timeliness, which can often be conflicting when a customer's due date is approaching. I believe I have both the skills and the temperament to maintain high standards under pressure.

I look forward to an opportunity to meet with you to further discuss my qualifications and your needs for the job. I will call you next week to arrange an appointment at your convenience. Thank you for your consideration.

Sincerely,

Hunter Bottjer

KEVIN SHANNON

P.O. Box 231, Bakersfield, CA 93301 / 805-555-9721

Mr. John Verbortt
Personnel Manager
Simmonds Manufacturing
2351 Frontage Road
Los Angeles, CA 90012

Dear Mr. Verbortt:

I am writing in reply to your advertisement in the *Los Angeles Times,* Sunday edition, for an engineering department coordinator.

I will soon be relocating to Los Angeles, where I hope to obtain a position as challenging as my current employment with Industrial Manufacturing, Inc., of Bakersfield. From the time I was hired, I took advantage of each opportunity for new responsibilities and challenges.

The position description in the newspaper indicated that the position carried opportunities for educational training and advancement. Over the past 10 years, I have taken 36 credit hours in continuing education courses to keep abreast of developments in the field. I am extremely interested in further enhancing my knowledge and skills in the area of applied engineering.

I bring to this position an extensive amount of classroom as well as practical, on-the-job training and experience, as well as several years of supervisory experience. My most recent promotion, to the role of National Coordinator for the corporation's P.A.R. system (Parts Action Request), has increased my experience with maintaining the detailed, precise communications needed in this critical aspect of manufacturing.

I will be in Los Angeles for the first two weeks of December, and would like to visit Simmonds Manufacturing to talk with you further about the position and my qualifications. I will call you next week to arrange a time at your convenience.

Thank you for your consideration.

Sincerely,

Kevin Shannon

1222 Washington Avenue
Wilmington, DE 19805

D.S.W. Industries
PO Box 664
Wilmington, DE 19803

Dear Sir or Madam:

Eager to pursue a career in engineering or urban planning, I am interested in the in-house public works inspector training position advertised in the May 19, 1994 *Gazette.*

As a recent graduate of the University of Delaware's Civil Engineering program, I possess the required academic and work experience. While pursuing my degree I consistently chose classes that expanded my structural and ECS knowledge beyond that required. I also took courses in public planning, geology, geography and landscape architecture to complete a minor in Environmental Studies. I have some construction experience through such classes as Design/Build and my drafting, design, and public relations skills were enhanced through a practicum experience with a local architectural firm and a summer internship with the Port of Delaware engineering division.

I am currently employed as an Engineering Specialist with the Port and am interested in other positions that would expand my knowledge and experience. My enclosed resume outlines additional skills and qualifications that would help me make a strong contribution to D.S.W. Industries. I am hard working and eager to learn, with good communication and people skills. I work well in team situations and require limited supervision.

I would greatly appreciate an opportunity to talk with you and further demonstrate how I could effectively fulfill your needs. I can be reached at the phone number below, by message before 5:30 p.m. or personally in the evenings. I look forward to hearing from you. Thank you for your time and consideration.

Sincerely,

Suzette W. Palmerson
(302) 555-2385

J. K. Norris
88 Marshall St. W.
Williston, ND 58801
(701) 555-2338

Personnel Division
Weston/Havens, Inc.
745 N.W. Wall Street
P.O. Box 218, Dept. PE 8
Denver, CO 80209

RE: Employment in Environmental/Waste Management (Hazardous/ Solid Waste)/Regulation Compliance/Business Development

    I am pleased to submit my resume in response to your advertised positions in the latest edition of <u>Engineering Update</u>. It outlines my experience in industrial and hazardous waste management, regulations (U.S. and Canadian), compliance and environmental technology.

    A professional engineer (P.Eng.) in chemical engineering with an M.B.A., I offer over 14 years of experience, including environmental technology, project management, technical standards development and high tech manufacturing. Most recently I held a position as a project manager of Environmental Technology at the EPA. Prior to the EPA I worked for 7 years at Pantheon Canada, a subsidiary of the Pantheon Co. of Lexington, Mass., taking care of industrial wastes, effluent treatment, recycling and regulation compliance (Reg-309, Clean Air Act, hazardous wastes, and MISA).

    Positions Desired: Senior engineering/project management
    Salary Desired: $60,000 range, but negotiable
    Locations: Open but prefer southwest, southeast or south-central U.S.

    I can be reached by phone at the above number for messages and will return your call promptly. I am happy to make arrangements to travel to Denver to meet with you and discuss the position further. Thank you for your consideration, and I look forward to talking with you soon.

Sincerely,

J.K. Norris, P.Eng., M.B.A.

E. JOSEPH BRINDLEY
3553 43rd Street West
Katy, Texas 77450
Work: (713) 555-0988
Home: (713) 555-3387

Mr. Jerry Herrold
President
Herrold Employment Enterprises
P.O. Box 2247
Dallas, Texas 75233

Dear Mr. Herrold:

I am interested in teaming up with your recruiting firm to accomplish an effective search for an environmental engineering position. My objective is to join an engineering services firm specializing in remedial investigations and feasibility studies — a company with opportunities ranging from initial assessment to implementation.

My background includes experience in formation evaluations, stratigraphic profiling, borehole geophysical surveys, ground-water analysis, and data acquisition and processing. Environmental knowledge and experience include:
- Storage, transportation, and survey of radioactive sources including attendant recordkeeping.
- Handling, storage, and transportation of explosives and explosive materials. Familiar with RCRA, CERCLA, SARA, TSCA, NRC, ATF, DOT, and similar regulations and regulating agencies.
- Scientific analysis of borehole geophysical data and the application of interpretation to properly describe hydrogeologic conditions.
- Market development activities including client studies and market assessments.
- Preparing and presenting significant presentations to senior management.

Please review my background relative to your current search assignments and contact me if you would like to talk further. I can be reached at (713) 555-0988 during working hours.

Sincerely,

E. Joseph Brindley

Enclosure

BENSON C. TUCKER   2114 NW Fremont Ave., Seattle, WA 98003 (206) 555-7712

ConMac Construction, Inc.
21 SW Pioneer St., Suite E
Seattle, WA 98002

Dear Sir:

I am writing in response to an engineering technician position advertised in the August 15 <u>Post-Intelligencer</u>. I am interested in learning more about the position, and would like to submit the enclosed resume in application. I believe my experience and qualifications fulfill your requirements to perform the job.

As you can see from my resume, I have a background in engineering, construction and earth science. My most recent position as a lab technician and field representative for a core analysis lab has exposed me to the evaluation of the physical characteristics of rock cores using a variety of technical testing equipment in the laboratory. I have also demonstrated my ability to coordinate and organize projects in the field under a variety of working conditions with little supervision.

My position as a framing foreman for a west coast construction firm provided seven years of hands-on experience in carpentry and construction methods. In addition, I oversaw subcontractors, transferred blueprints to building layout, directed carpenter crews, and was largely responsible for ensuring that construction was carried out in compliance with building codes.

I enjoy working in a lab environment and also welcome any opportunity to work in the field. I have proven myself to be reliable, motivated, hardworking, and able to communicate comfortably with clients and coworkers.

Thank you for considering my qualifications. I would appreciate the opportunity to talk with you in person.

Sincerely,

Benson C. Tucker

TriWeld, Inc.
P.O. BOX 254
St. Paul, MN 55123
(612) 555-4493

Dear Hiring Executive:
Re: Your ad in the *Minnesotan* of 7/18 for a Construction Inspector Trainee

I am currently Manufacturing Production Manager at Plastimade in St. Paul, a manufacturer of heavy duty vinyl products for industrial, government, and consumer markets. While I have been successful here in improving productivity, I would like to return to a metals fabrication organization, which has been my prior specialty.

At STANLEY INDUSTRIAL TOOLS, my title was Production Supervisor, with extensive experience in multiple department, multiple shift operations. My responsibilities included forecasting; planning of products, equipment, and manpower; inventory management; hiring and training; and directing production operations. I have directly managed up to 78 employees and multimillion-dollar department budgets.

I have an A.S. degree in Electronics Technology and ongoing management training courses taken during my 20 years of direct production line experience. Through my personal "continuous improvement" philosophy, I have enhanced efficiency while lowering costs. For example:

• Reduced product lead times by five weeks, inventory by 20%, and customer back-orders by 98%.

• Managed five product improvement teams implementing modem quality management techniques; i.e., SPC and ISO 9002 international quality standards. Realized more than $200,000 in annual savings.

• Developed the manufacturing process for 29 models of "industry's best" torque wrenches. Implemented two wage classifications, yielding 11% labor savings.

I am an achievement-oriented team leader, dedicated to continuous improvement. If you need a "get it done" type of manager, with a modern team approach and a proven record of accomplishment, perhaps we should talk. If you would like to discuss current or future possibilities within your company, you may reach me at the phone number and address below. I will call you in a few days to inquire about a convenient time for a meeting.

Thank you for your consideration.

Roger W. Fenton
223 S. Cameron Drive
St. Paul, MN 55223
(612) 555-0443

Personnel Manager
Binder Engineering, Inc.
Box 1124, Dept. E
New Orleans, LA 70123

Dear Personnel Manager:

I am a recent graduate of Oregon State University with a degree in Civil Engineering. I am seeking an entry level Civil Engineering position in your firm. I feel my education and work experience have prepared me to be a strong asset to your company.

I have placed in the top 10 in the American Institute of Steel Construction bridge design competition for two years. I have been an active participant in the design and fabrication of the bridges, and this year I was in charge of the fabrication team, consisting of ten people.

While completing my degree, I worked for Crowd Management Services, a security company, assigning personnel to perform various tasks. Also, as a landscape contractor, I followed city codes concerning the installation of residential irrigation systems, built small non-engineered retaining walls, and worked with concrete construction.

In my design courses, I gained experience in the use various manuals: the ASTM, LRFD, NDSI, ACI, and the UBC. These courses provided me with practical knowledge that will enable me to properly design structures. Contracts and Specifications courses concentrated on contract documents, bidding requirements, contract conditions, contract forms, specifications, and drawings. Engineering Economic Planning focused on economical land use, zoning, selection of multiple alternatives, benefit-to-cost analysis, and replacement analysis.

I am familiar with several engineering computer programs, such as ETABS and Quattro Pro. I know how to write programs using GW Basic. I am currently enrolled in a course on AutoCAD Release 12.

Please find the enclosed resume which summarizes my qualifications. I look forward to further discussing my qualifications with you, at your convenience. Please contact me at 555-4450 (message). Thank you for your time and consideration.

Sincerely,

Jason Swift
2216 Marshall Heights Road, Apt. G3
New Orleans, LA 70112
(504) 555-4450

115 Twining Street, #451
Baltimore, MD 21209

Sundstrand Enterprises, LTD
P.O. Box 225
Baltimore, MD 21218

Dear Sundstrand Enterprises:

In response to your recent advertisement for Engineering Inspectors,
I would like to submit the enclosed resume and letters of
recommendation for your consideration.

I am especially interested in your company, as it combines
engineering with construction. Having recently returned to college to
complete a bachelor's degree in construction engineering, I am eager
to begin new challenges. My twelve years of experience in the
construction field, including major commercial and residential
projects, should be an important asset in working with Sundstrand
Enterprises.

My mathematical and record-keeping skills are strong and have been a
major part of my work as project inspector and as a general
contractor. Good communication is an essential element in any
successful project. I have weathered union strikes, unfriendly
takeovers and reorganizations with satisfactory resolutions and the
project completed.

I would appreciate an opportunity to arrange an interview at your
convenience. I can be reached for messages at 301-555-9985, and I will
return your call promptly. I look forward to talking with you, and
thank you for your consideration.

Sincerely,

Andy Freeman

Enc.: resume

17 West Barley Mow
Boston, Mass. 02129

Mr. John Patterson
Director of Personnel
Hall, Winston & Merck, Architects
2251 W. Pyncheon
Boston, Mass. 02113

Dear Mr. Patterson:

In the January 30 edition of the <u>Globe</u>, your firm ran an ad for a Construction Inspector Trainee. I submit the enclosed resume and letters of reference in application for this position.

I hold a Bachelor of Science Degree in Civil Engineering Technology from the Massachusetts Institute of Technology. While pursuing my degree, I had the opportunity to study many areas associated with civil engineering, including materials testing (soil, concrete, and asphalt), math (through applied calculus), and construction management.

Along with my education, I have experience working with an architectural/engineering firm producing site, foundation, and floor plans, as well as roof systems and connection details. Recently, I had the opportunity to assist in the construction of residential and small commercial structures for an independent contractor.

I would like to meet with you to answer any additional questions that you might have regarding my qualifications. I can be reached at the address listed above or at (617) 555-2448. Thank you, and I look forward to hearing from you soon.

Sincerely,

Tamana Clarendon

Enclosures: Resume
References (3)

ROBERTA LOEB
34 Michigan Drive
Des Moines, IA 50317

Mr. Joshua Sellwood
Magnussen Engineering
17 West Hallows Ave., Suite 334
Des Moines, IA 50309

Dear Joshua:

It was very good to be able to talk with you about opportunities with
Environmental Associates. I came away from our discussion feeling as if I'd
found an ideal match for both my interests and qualifications. Enclosed is my
resume outlining my professional experience, as well as a list of professional
references for your consideration.

As we discussed, I am a registered civil engineer with over seven years of
civil/environmental marketing experience in the environmental construction
products industry with Semlar Environmental Systems (Semlar structural
geogrids) and Crown Zellerbach Corporation (nonwoven geotextiles). Prior
experience includes nine years as a project/construction manager for Bechtel
Engineering and six years as a project/refinery engineer in the oil industry.

My professional objective now is a regional marketing and/or technical support
position within the private sector. My extensive contacts in the Midwest with
environmental engineering consultants, regulatory agencies, and landfill
owners/operators will offer the prospect of generating new business for your firm.

Thank you kindly for your assistance. I look forward to talking with you further.

Sincerely,

Roberta Loeb, P.E.

Enclosure

BRANDON NICKERSON, P.E.
667 Hurst Ave.
St. Louis, MO 63121

Susan W. Coolidge
Vice President
Simmonds Technology, Inc.
Rt. 5, Box 1265
St. Louis, MO 63102

Dear Ms. Coolidge:

I am sending you my resume for your consideration for any suitable openings which your firm may have at the present time.

I believe my experience in many facets of the environmental field—including project design, procurement, scheduling and construction—will allow me to make a significant contribution to your operations. Also, my extensive background in electrical and process control systems has given me a well rounded understanding of most chemical, thermal and physical processes.

In addition to my engineering management and technical skills, I have had considerable experience in project development, new business development and the implementation of new technology. During the past seven years I have also had extensive experience in the solid waste management field with in-depth involvement in medical, industrial and municipal waste handling, incineration, energy recovery and pollution control projects.

I am available for immediate employment and can travel extensively or relocate as required. I look forward to hearing from you and learning more about any current openings for which I am qualified. Thank you for your consideration.

Yours sincerely,

Brandon Nickerson

Enclosure: Resume

Shawn Seeley
22 W. Davis St.
Saginaw, Michigan 48603
Tel: (517) 555-2625

Abel Maxwell
Senior Engineer
Patterby Industrial, Inc.
345 Frontage Road
Saginaw, MI 48602

Dear Mr. Maxwell:

Please accept the enclosed resume as my application for the recently announced engineering technologist position at Patterby Industrial.

As a recent graduate of the UM Engineering Program in engineering technology, I can assure you that I have been trained by some of the very best — both among my professors at UM and among the professional engineers from major corporations throughout the Midwest who provided on-campus seminars in the latest in engineering technology.

As a participant in the annual Engineering Technology Competition, I won second prize for two consecutive years, and was part of the team that won first prize this past year. The competition fosters independence, innovation, and team work. You will find that I am an excellent team player, but that I have the ability to lead when the situation demands.

I would like to arrange an opportunity to visit Patterby Industrial to see your operations and learn more about your requirements for this position. I am eager to match my training and abilities to your needs.

I look forward to hearing from you soon. I can be reached at the number above most afternoons, and messages can be left at any time. Thank you for your consideration.

Sincerely,

Shawn Seeley

Darius G.W. Harms
3485 Plainfield Road
Lincoln, Nebraska 68573
402-555-9287

Jonathan Parker
Engineering Division Director
State of Nebraska
P.O. Box 5678
Lincoln, Nebraska 68570

Dear Mr. Parker:

Please accept this letter and the enclosed resume in application for the Engineering Supervisor position announced February 25.

I believe my extensive background in structural and mechanical engineering meets or exceeds the qualifications you are looking for. I have served both as a senior engineer and as an engineering supervisor with responsibility for 120 workers.

For my part, I would like to put my expertise and experience to work for the benefit of public works projects, where safety and quality form the guiding values, as stated in your position description. Too often in the corporate world, the demand for higher profit margins takes precedence over innovative developments and worker safety. My experience in this field, however, has given me the ability to achieve desired results in the most efficient manner possible, thus cutting costs and increasing productivity.

Please review the enclosed resume and call me at the number above. I would very much like to talk with you about the position and what my experience can bring to your department.

Yours truly,

Darius Harms

Human Resources Director
Search Committee: Senior Technical Editor
Merrick Engineering, Inc.
P.O. Box 223
Rutland, Vermont 05702

To the Members of the Search Committee:

Enclosed please find my application for the technical writer/editor position currently available at Merrick's Rutland office.

From the Environmental Computing Center to the new University Theatre and an endowed professorship in integrated circuit design, I have written, edited, and coordinated more than 150 grant proposals for many of the University of Vermont's most significant projects. As Proposal Writer for the University's Foundation and Development office, I work closely with vice presidents, deans, directors, and faculty to present their projects to both lay and technical audiences. I directly supervise two staff members and a student assistant, and coordinate the efforts of others involved in the grant-writing and fund-raising process within the University.

My graduate work in English and undergraduate studies in pre-medicine at Stanford have prepared me to write with ease on a variety of topics. I've edited complicated research presentations for many of the University's premier scientists while also working with leading scholars in the humanities to prepare fund-raising documents for various cultural programs.

My experience as a free-lance writer, graphic designer, and photographer further qualify me for this position. Two of my recent publications present biographies and in-depth research abstracts on scientists featured in *Nobel Prize Winners: Physiology and Medicine*.

Your prospectus requested salary requirements. As my primary interest in the position is in the challenges it offers to put my skills to good use for a company that has a strong international reputation for excellence, I would be satisfied should the proposed remuneration meet my current gross annual income of $45,000, which includes salary and benefits.

I will be out of town until the 19th, after which I will be happy to meet with you. I would value the opportunity to join the strong and growing team at Merrick, and I appreciate your review of my application.

Sincerely,

Amanda Wentworth
26 West Parade Drive
Rutland, Vermont 05702
802-555-9847

1233 Mission Street
San Pablo, California 98329

Personnel Director
Bakersfield & Associates
Box 123
San Pablo, California 98332

Dear Director:

Please accept the enclosed resume in application for the position of Engineering Sales Specialist, which was advertised in the *San Francisco Chronicle* last week.

I've worked as a civil engineer for the past eight years and have gained tremendous insight into the issues involved in marketing engineering services on an international basis.

Early in my career, I gained some valuable experience as the Engineering Sales Specialist for Shell Oil Company. In this position, I worked with manufacturers and small business owners to coordinate efforts for fuel efficiency and cost savings. The marketing and sales program that resulted was the most successful in the company's history.

During my graduate program at MIT, I worked closely with several faculty members in consultation with a major technology manufacturer to recast the company's image and stimulate sales in a slogging economy. The strategic planning sessions with corporate executives provided a tremendous on-the-job training opportunity for me as a graduate student, and the project achieved the desired results.

My inquiries have revealed that your firm has a strong reputation for excellence and innovation that makes me eager to bring my skills in strategic planning and market analysis to work for Bakersfield & Associates.

I would appreciate an opportunity to discuss the position with you further. Please call me at 213/555-0812, where messages may be left if I am personally unavailable.

Thank you for your consideration.

Sincerely,

Donna Everson

Jane Bessington • 18 West Court Street • Shreveport, Louisiana 71102 • 318-555-6510

Jane Flanagan
Director of Personnel
AT&T
9595 Mansfield
Shreveport, LA 71130

Dear Ms. Flanagan:

I am writing in response to the advertised electronics engineering position. Please accept the enclosed resume in application.

I was particularly attracted to this position because of my previous experience as an electronics engineering technician with ACI and Associates in New Orleans, where I was officially an Engineer-In-Training while preparing for professional licensing. I have completed all necessary courses and examinations, and will have confirmation of my license by next week.

AT&T's commitment to further educational training is an essential factor in my choosing to apply for this position. The dynamic nature of this field, and the number of individuals working toward new and innovative technology, both within AT&T and in other agencies, mean that vast amounts of valuable information need to be reviewed in order to stay on top. As you will notice in my resume, I have also attended additional training seminars to keep current with this rapidly changing field.

I believe my credentials and commitment to innovation and development will make me an excellent candidate for this position. I look forward to talking with you soon.

Sincerely,

Jane Bessington

Abdul Gassazi Murza
224 West Fourth Street
Albany, New York 12211
518/555-6428

Dr. Lewis J. Stone
Director
Aeromechanical Engineering Division
McDonnell Douglas Helicopter Company
4645 South Ash Avenue
Tempe, Arizona 85282

Dear Dr. Stone:

After meeting with you at the American Institute of Aeronautics and Astronautics convention last week in Phoenix, I am delighted to write now in application for an entry-level position with your aeromechanics engineering division. Our discussion was most valuable in providing information about McDonnell Douglas's helicopter branch, and I am intrigued to become part of such an exciting operation.

As a graduate student at Boston's Wentworth Institute, my focus was primarily on the design and construction of military jets. I was able to apply the principles of aeronautics and aeromechanics to my work as a research assistant on a project for testing the aeroelasticity of materials for safer, more efficient production of supersonic jets. The project resulted in a patented new technology, which is currently being employed in the construction of several new jets for the U.S. Air Force.

I would like to visit your facilities and talk with you further about what I can bring to this position. If possible, I would appreciate approximately 10 days notice, so that I can make appropriate travel arrangements.

Thank you for your consideration. I look forward to talking with you again soon.

Best regards,

Abdul Murza

2276 La Center Blvd.
Gainesville, FL 32601

R.W. Matson
Matson & Carter Enterprises
One Commercial Parkway East
Tampa, FL 32200

Dear R.W. Matson:

In response to your recent advertisement in the *Florida Herald,* I am writing to apply for the position as quality control engineer. My resume, enclosed, indicates the extensive training and experience I have behind me in the field of quality assurance and quality control. My strengths include an ability to work successfully with people—from top department managers and CEOs to entry-level engineering technicians and production line personnel. I am dependable, dedicated to quality, and have a positive "teamwork" attitude.

My professional experience has primarily been in the nuclear engineering field. The career change from the nuclear industry will enable me to bring a fresh perspective to all of your energy-related clients because of the essential element of safety and quality control in this exacting field.

I look forward to meeting with you at your earliest convenience. You may reach me at 407/555-2203, ext. 1945 during working hours, and at 407/555-3090 evenings and weekends. Thank you for your time and consideration.

With best regards,

K.J. Butters

Draycott Engineering, Inc.
Center Building Complex
Suite 221
5377 W. Carver
Seattle, WA 98002

To the Director of Personnel:

The enclosed resume and letters of recommendation are being submitted in application for the Assistant Project Manager's position with your company, announced in the September 20 edition of *Seattle Business Week*.

I have recently relocated to the Seattle area and am looking forward to taking on new challenges in my engineering career. Most recently I worked as a public works inspector, primarily involved with inspection of civil engineering projects and assisting with project planning. My previous positions were as an assistant project manager for a major construction corporation and as an engineering technician for a local government agency.

My experience covers all areas of project management, including design, planning, budgeting, scheduling, and personnel management. I am available to travel, as required, but prefer to keep Seattle as my primary base.

I will call you next week to arrange a time to discuss the position -- and my credentials -- with you at greater length. If you have any questions, please call me at the number below. I look forward to hearing from you.

Sincerely,

Susan G. Carter
1983 Madison, SE
Bellevue, WA 98008
(206) 555-2283

VGM CAREER BOOKS

CAREER DIRECTORIES
Careers Encyclopedia
Dictionary of Occupational Titles
Occupational Outlook Handbook

CAREERS FOR
Animal Lovers
Bookworms
Computer Buffs
Crafty People
Culture Lovers
Environmental Types
Film Buffs
Foreign Language Aficionados
Good Samaritans
Gourmets
History Buffs
Kids at Heart
Nature Lovers
Night Owls
Number Crunchers
Plant Lovers
Shutterbugs
Sports Nuts
Travel Buffs

CAREERS IN
Accounting; Advertising;
Business; Child Care;
Communications; Computers;
Education; Engineering;
the Environment; Finance;
Government; Health Care;
High Tech; Journalism; Law;
Marketing; Medicine;
Science; Social &
Rehabilitation Services

CAREER PLANNING
Admissions Guide to Selective Business Schools
Beating Job Burnout
Beginning Entrepreneur
Career Planning & Development for College Students & Recent Graduates
Career Change

Careers Checklists
Cover Letters They Don't Forget
Executive Job Search Strategies
Guide to Basic Cover Letter Writing
Guide to Basic Resume Writing
Guide to Temporary Employment
Job Interviews Made Easy
Joyce Lain Kennedy's Career Book
Out of Uniform
Resumes Made Easy
Slam Dunk Resumes
Successful Interviewing for College Seniors
Time for a Change

CAREER PORTRAITS
Animals	Nursing
Cars	Sports
Computers	Teaching
Music	Travel

GREAT JOBS FOR
Communications Majors
English Majors
Foreign Language Majors
History Majors
Psychology Majors

HOW TO
Approach an Advertising Agency and Walk Away with the Job You Want
Bounce Back Quickly After Losing Your Job
Choose the Right Career
Find Your New Career Upon Retirement
Get & Keep Your First Job
Get Hired Today
Get into the Right Business School
Get into the Right Law School
Get People to Do Things Your Way
Have a Winning Job Interview

Hit the Ground Running in Your New Job
Improve Your Study Skills
Jump Start a Stalled Career
Land a Better Job
Launch Your Career in TV News
Make the Right Career Moves
Market Your College Degree
Move from College into a Secure Job
Negotiate the Raise You Deserve
Prepare a Curriculum Vitae
Prepare for College
Run Your Own Home Business
Succeed in College
Succeed in High School
Write a Winning Resume
Write Successful Cover Letters
Write Term Papers & Reports
Write Your College Application Essay

OPPORTUNITIES IN
This extensive series provides detailed information on nearly 150 individual career fields.

RESUMES FOR
Advertising Careers
Banking and Financial Careers
Business Management Careers
College Students & Recent Graduates
Communications Careers
Education Careers
Engineering Careers
Environmental Careers
50 + Job Hunters
Health and Medical Careers
High School Graduates
High Tech Careers
Law Careers
Midcareer Job Changes
Sales and Marketing Careers
Scientific and Technical Careers
Social Service Careers
The First-Time Job Hunter

VGM Career Horizons
a division of *NTC Publishing Group*
4255 West Touhy Avenue
Lincolnwood, Illinois 60646-1975